FORGOTTEN STOIC : 1

I Went in Search of Myself

A New Edition of the Fragments of Heraclitus

WAKING CRANE PRESS

ISBN: 978-1092317160

Ed. MICHAEL S. PRATT

FORGOTTEN STOIC SERIES

This Title:

Forgotten Stoic : Heraclitus — I Went in Search of Myself
A New Edition of the Fragments of Heraclitus of Ephesus
First published May 2019
Second edition March 2024
ISBN: 9781092317160
By: Heraclitus; Michael S. Pratt: Translation, Editing, Notes

Other Titles in the Forgotten Stoic Series:

Forgotten Stoic : Solon of Athens — Wisdom of Solon and Complete Poetry
Also includes: The Seven Sages of Greece
Timeless Wisdom of the Founders of Western Civilization
By: Solon; Seven Sages; Michael S. Pratt: Translation, Editing, Notes
First published February 2016
Second edition March 2024
ISBN: 9781070115283

Forgotten Stoic : Plotinus — Strain and See
First published March 2024
By: Plotinus; Michael S. Pratt: Introduction, Editing
ISBN: 9798879397413

All rights reserved. No part of this publication may be reproduced in any form or by any means without permission of the publisher.

> THE
> ETERNAL
> WAKEFULNESS
> OF THE CRANE
> FALLING ASLEEP
> THE STONE FALLS
> INTO THE WATER
> WAKING HER
> AGAIN
>
> ☀

All things arise and pass away.

But the awakened awake forever.

Buddha

Contents

Introduction—The Path

THE FRAGMENTS OF HERACLITUS OF EPHESUS

A Note about the Logos   Page 151

Context, Notes and Commentary   Page 158

Further Reading   Page 219

Introduction—The Path

Dear Reader,

You have opened this book and I hope you will experience something similar to how I felt on first encountering Heraclitus' words. They stunned and shocked me to my core and also at the same time gave me hope in a way that I cannot adequately describe. 'How is it possible to not always have known these words?' was a constantly recurring thought. A piercing, urgent reality as well as a glimpse of an all-encompassing vision of the universe opened up. "Our soul," says Heraclitus, "is a spark of stellar essence." The works of Heraclitus, these fragments, touched me as no other writings or works of art have — they do so today and every day.

Heraclitus has been called the first Stoic, even though he lived generations before the founding of the Stoic School, and the Stoics have been called the true Heracliteans of antiquity. Perhaps you have read the name Heraclitus in some of the most influential writings in Stoicism, which is how I first learned about him. Heraclitus is mentioned in Epictetus' *Manual* and by Marcus Aurelius in his *Meditations*. Both these Stoic teachers lived and worked more than five centuries after Heraclitus and deeply respected him as a great sage.

Epictetus simply called Heraclitus "Divine" as we read in the following passage, in Chapter 15 of the *Manual*, also known as *The Enchiridion*:

> *Remember that in life you must behave like at a dinner party. Is anything brought around to you? Put out your hand and take your share with moderation. Does it pass you by? Don't stop it. Is is not yet come? Don't stretch your desire towards it, but wait till it reaches you. Do this with regard to children, to a wife, to public posts, to riches and you will eventually be a worthy partner of the feasts of the Gods.*

And if you don't even take the things which are set before you, but are even able to reject them, then you will not only be a partner at the feasts of the Gods, but also of their empire. For by doing this, Diogenes, Heraclitus, and others like them, deservedly became, and were called, Divine.

Marcus Aurelius wrote in his private notebook, now known as his *Meditations* to remind himself always of Heraclitus' words:

Always remember the sayings of Heraclitus...and think too of him who forgets wither the way leads, and that men quarrel with that with which they are most constantly in communion, the Reason which governs the universe, and the things which they daily meet with seem to them strange, and consider that we ought not to act and speak as if we were asleep...

(From Book 4, translation: George Long).

With such significant references should we not find out more about Heraclitus' life and study his writings?

Heraclitus "flourished," as the old Greeks write, a generation or two after the time of Solon, Thales, Bias and others of the Seven Sages that were so influential breathing new life into Greek civilization. Born in Ephesus, Ionia, [Asia Minor] he lived there approximately from 544 to 484 BCE (Before Common Era). This is the time of the earliest Greek philosophers, the First Philosophers, often referred to as the Presocratics.

There are very few known facts about Heraclitus' life. He came from an aristocratic family and refused to serve Persian conqueror King Darius, who had asked Heraclitus to teach him philosophy. But it is for example not known if he studied with another philosopher, was part of a school, or if he had students during his lifetime. What is known is that he wrote a book about the universe and man's position in it which became famous during his time and very influential for hundreds of years thereafter. It had tremendous impact on one of the founding figures of the early Stoic School, Cleanthes, the successor to Zeno.

The Book of Heraclitus, originally dedicated and safeguarded in the Great Temple of Artemis in Ephesus, no longer exists. The Temple of Artemis, one of the seven wonders of the ancient world, was burned down—a most portentous omen—at the same time as the birth of Alexander the Great. But copies existed probably until well in the Neoplatonist times, 2nd and 3rd century CE (Common Era).

Now only some 130 mostly short, enigmatic fragments of Heraclitus writings remain and have been preserved, and these through historians and philosophers over a time period spanning centuries after his death.

Heraclitus' words (the fragments are the first prose in Greek civilization) have been considered difficult to penetrate—riddling, obscure, oracular—and have inspired numerous philosophers and writers to think, comment and write about them. From Socrates, Plato and Aristotle to the Stoics: Cleanthes, Epictetus, Marcus Aurelius, Seneca, to the Neoplatonists such as Plotinus, to the Early Christian fathers, to Marsilio Ficino in the Renaissance, and later to Goethe, Nietzsche, Heidegger and T.S. Eliot, and now they are for us here today.

Historian Diogenes Laërtius, in the third century CE (Common Era) quotes the following on how to read Heraclitus in his *Life and Opinions of Eminent Philosophers*:

Do not be in too great a hurry to get to the end of Heraclitus the Ephesian's book: the path is hard to travel. Gloom is there and darkness devoid of light. But if an initiate be your guide, the path shines brighter than sunlight.

Beyond the difficulty of being hard to traverse—its legendary obscurity (and more on that later)—any project today about the remaining fragments of the oracle that is Heraclitus, presents some additional interlocking issues: authenticity and context of the fragments. All this is necessarily part of any translation and interpretation. Then there is the question of a meaningful ordering of the fragments.

The latter issue, trying to arrange the fragments into a meaningful order as it could have been in the original book, is almost destined to failure because the remaining fragments do not always neatly fit into one grouping or another based on themes selected by the commentator. For the modern reader not intimately familiar with the Greek language there are other hurdles we hope to address in this edition of the fragments.

Most scholarly writings about Heraclitus use a numbering system for the fragments based on the 19th and 20th century scholars Hermann Diels and Walther Kranz (the Diels-Kranz numbering system from *Die Fragmente der Vorsokratiker*, first published in 1903). This, along with what is often their own arrangement or numbering system and the unfortunate fact that many studies do not even translate the fragments or simply refer to a fragment number alone, makes it so our study often requires two, three or more books and dictionaries open, constantly consulting the concordances tables.

The Diels-Kranz numbering system expressly disclaims that it reflects the original order in Heraclitus' book (except for Fragment 1) but is in our view still practical. It is adopted here, just to make it easier to consult the fragments themselves when reading the many writings about Heraclitus, and that is one of the main purposes of this book.

Another pertinent issue, in our view, is the distraction in most editions of having the commentary immediately imposing on, taking over and frequently obscuring the meaning of the actual fragments. Heraclitus' utterances are often short with multiple layers of meaning and therefore require intentionality while reading them, with attention, time and space. Hence in this edition, each fragment stands alone on a single page, so that in a practical way we can contemplate them a little more easily.

As to interpretation and translation, the aim for this new edition is to give voice to a current understanding how it came to be that Epictetus considered Heraclitus to have become "divine."

"Divine" we understand to mean man or woman as an awakened being who has fully realized their potential in the same way we consider Buddha or Lao Tsu (both roughly contemporaries of Heraclitus) to be enlightened masters. In the words of Epictetus: a worthy partner of the empire of the Gods. In short, a God.

Endeavoring to heed the words of Heraclitus is to go "in search of ourselves" and being mindful that our attempts to "try his words and works" will prove to us that in our current state of awareness we are "shown to be without experience" and will "forever fail to understand."

We agree with Diogenes Laërtius: the path was—and must always remain—hard to travel. Gloom and darkness are acute and very real because any sincere attempt to approach the work of Heraclitus reveals to us, more than anything else, our own total and utter oblivion.

Heraclitus at once points to the *Logos*—that divine cosmic ordering principle—*and* to our near total inability to be a meaningful part thereof: for us to reach and be in a state of conscious awareness. We are deeply asleep and we will forever fail to understand how we can and need to awaken. And we will fail to understand it even after being told about it as Heraclitus concludes from the very first fragment. Just reading and trying to grasp the fragments intellectually is clearly not enough. We have to apply and live what is offered through these words. What this perhaps can mean will be discussed in the second part of this book where we provide some thoughts, context and further reading suggestions related to the fragments.

The theme of sleep and waking (our current state of oblivion but somewhere within it our *possible* state of higher awareness) recurs with alarming frequency in Heraclitus' fragments in colorful imagery and is the point of departure for this book, just as it was a constant reminder for Marcus Aurelius.

More than anything else we need to understand our current condition of sleep and we must understand it deeply. And we must be radical about it, that is to say, we must realize these fragments are written *about us*, and *addressed to us* directly, mercilessly. He exhorts *us* to "Rise up and become wakeful watchers of living men and corpses."

But if we miss the vital point that in our present state we live, feel and think in a state of almost absolute oblivion we become like most philosophers and scholars merely taking Heraclitus' words to have meaning about somebody else and something outside of ourselves, never considering that *we* have to change within. And so we end up only proving Heraclitus' saying that "much learning does not teach understanding." We are then easily lost in the process of continual digging and sifting through the material trying to parse out some theoretical meaning or nuance, all the while reducing the fragments to the point where they lose their immediate and urgent connection to us. The "fairest world order" thus constructed in our imagination will be nothing but a "heap of random sweepings" as Heraclitus warns.

From the opening fragment and throughout the works, Heraclitus exhorts that we "hear like the deaf" and "are without comprehension." We are "absent while present." We (not someone else, but *we*) are the sleepers, the drunkards, the dead imagining to be alive. The sparks and small fires we manage to kindle in this process of waking up to our own Divine Fire are soon extinguished.

So before we can be guided by Heraclitus along the path we have to come to terms with the fact that he points to *us*, and describes *us*, in the fragments as "cattle stuffing themselves," and "asses choosing garbage over gold."

We are the "swine delighting in mire" and *we* are the "chickens bathing in dust," as further described by Heraclitus. So *we* must accept the "blows by which all beasts are guided," (yes, *we* are the beasts) and *we* must let go of our own opinions. He instructs *us* to "douse our hubris faster and more thoroughly than a raging fire."

No matter the weariness that Heraclitus describes and accepts as part of this struggle (and *we* must too), we have to start again, and again, that long inner war: moment by moment to be beginners in search of ourselves, and to learn to re-cognite ourselves.

Rising from sleep, this time choosing gold over garbage.

THE FRAGMENTS
OF THE BOOK OF
HERACLITUS

This Logos holds eternal

Yet men forever fail to understand it

Both before hearing

And once they have heard it.

Although all things come to pass

According to this Logos, men,

When they try words and works such as I set forth,

Distinguishing the essence of things

And showing how it is,

They find themselves without experience.

They are oblivious to what they do while awake,

Just as they are oblivious while asleep.

Fragment 1

Although the Logos is present everywhere,

Men live as though their thinking was their own.

Fragment 2

The sun is the width of a human foot.

Fragment 3

Cattle delight in bitter vetch.

Fragment 4

They vainly try to purify themselves with blood

While defiled by blood,

As if one who had stepped in mud

Were to try to wash it off with mud;

He would be thought mad

If any man noticed him doing so.

Further, they pray to these statues,

As if one were to talk with houses;

Not recognizing what Gods and heroes really are.

Fragment 5

The sun is new every day.

Fragment 6

If all things became smoke,

The nostrils would discern them.

Fragment 7

All things come to pass through strife.

Counter-forces bring together,

From tones at variance,

Perfect harmony.

Fragment 8

Asses choose garbage over gold.

Fragment 9

Connections:

Things whole and not whole,

Things being brought together and brought apart,

Things in tune and out of tune,

Out of everything Unity,

And out of Unity All.

Fragment 10

All beasts are driven by blows.

Fragment 11

Upon those who are stepping into the same rivers

Different and again different waters flow.

Fragment 12

Swine delight in mire more than pure water.

Fragment 13

The initiation into the mysteries

Practiced among men

Is unholy.

Fragment 14

If it were not to Dionysus that they made the procession

And sung hymns to the shameful parts,

Their action would be most shameless;

But Hades and Dionysus are the same,

No matter how they rave and celebrate bacchic rites.

Fragment 15

How can one hide from that Light which never sets?

Fragment 16

Most men do not understand what they encounter.

They do not recognize what they experience.

But they do believe their own opinions.

Fragment 17

He who does not expect

Will not find out the unexpected;

For the Path is trackless

And unexplored.

Fragment 18

Not knowing how to listen

Neither can they speak.

Fragment 19

Once born,

They wish to live

And they meet their doom;

Leaving children behind

To become their doom

In turn.

Fragment 20

Death is what we see awake;

All we see asleep is sleep.

Fragment 21

Seekers of gold dig up much earth

And find but little.

Fragment 22

If not for these things,

Men would not know the name of Justice.

Fragment 23

Gods and men honor those slain in battle.

Fragment 24

Greater deaths win greater destinies.

Fragment 25

A man is kindled as a light in the night,

Having died, his sight extinguished.

Living,

He touches the dead in his sleep.

Awakened,

He touches the sleeper.

Fragment 26

There await men when they die

Whichever things they do not expect for themselves

Or even imagine.

Fragment 27

The most esteemed man

Holds fast to

Just imaginings.

Fragment 28a

The Goddess of Justice

Shall overtake the fabricators of lies

And their false witnesses.

Fragment 28b

The best choose one thing

In exchange for all:

Everlasting glory in place of mortal things;

While most men stuff themselves like cattle.

Fragment 29

The Cosmos

The same for all,

No God or man has made,

But it ever was, is, and will be:

Divine Fire

Kindled in measures

And going out in measures.

Fragment 30

The turnings of Fire:

First sea,

And of sea

Half is earth,

Half fiery wind

Such as forms the Stars.

Fragment 31a

Sea spreads out from earth,

Measuring the same amount it was

Before becoming earth.

Fragment 31b

One,

The only truly Wise,

Willing and Unwilling,

To be called by the name of Zeus.

Fragment 32

It is law also

To obey the counsel of one.

Fragment 33

Not comprehending they hear like the deaf.

This saying bears their witness:

Absent while present.

Fragment 34

Men who are lovers of wisdom

Must be good inquirers

Into many things.

Fragment 35

For souls it is death to become water,

For water it is death to become earth;

But out of earth water comes to be,

And out of water, Soul.

Fragment 36

Swine delight in mire,

Barnyard fowls in dust.

Fragment 37

Thales was an astronomer.

Fragment 38

In Priene there lived Bias, son of Teutames,

Whose Logos was worth more than the rest.

The citizens of Priene consecrated him a precinct

Called Teutameion;

He stated: *'Most men are bad.'*

Fragment 39

Much learning does not teach understanding.

Otherwise it would have taught Hesiod, Pythagoras,

Xenophanes and Hecataeus.

Fragment 40

Wisdom is the one thing:

To know the Will that steers all things through All.

Fragment 41

Homer deserves to be expelled from the contests

And beaten with a staff

And Archilochus likewise.

Fragment 42

Douse hubris

Faster and more thoroughly than a raging fire.

Fragment 43

The people must fight for their law

As for their city wall.

Fragment 44

You will not find out the limits of the Soul by going,

Even if you travel over every way,

So deep is its Logos.

Fragment 45

Conceit is a sacred disease.

Seeing is being deceived.

Fragment 46

Let us not speak casually about the most important matters.

Fragment 47

The name of the bow is life,

But its work is death.

Fragment 48

One man is as ten thousand to me

If he be the best.

Fragment 49

It is wise, then, for those who are listening,

Not to me,

But to the Logos,

To agree that all things are One.

Fragment 50

Men do not understand how what is brought apart

Comes together with itself;

There is a tuning,

Turning back on itself

Like that of the bow and the lyre.

Fragment 51

Lifetime is a child at play,

Moving pieces in a game.

Kingship belongs to the Child.

Fragment 52

War,

Father and King of all,

He renders some Gods, others men,

Some slaves,

Others free.

Fragment 53

Hidden harmony is superior to apparent.

Fragment 54

Whatever comes from sight, hearing,

Learning from experience:

This I prefer.

Fragment 55

Men are self-deceived

In their knowledge of apparent things.

Just as Homer

— Although the wisest of all the Greeks —

Was self-deceived by boys killing lice

When they riddled him:

'What we have seen and caught we leave behind

And what we have neither seen nor caught

We take with us.

Fragment 56

The teacher of most men is Hesiod.

It is him they know as knowing most,

A man who did not recognize day and night.

For they are one.

Fragment 57

Doctors

Cut and burn,

Complain they do not receive a worthy fee;

But produce the same result as the disease.

Fragment 58

Of the carding-roller,

The straight and the crooked way

Is one and the same.

Fragment 59

The way up

And the way down

Are one and the same.

Fragment 60

Sea:

The most pure and the most polluted water:

For fish — drinkable and life-sustaining;

For men — undrinkable and deadly.

Fragment 61

Immortals are mortal,

Mortals immortal,

Living the others' death,

Dead in the others' life.

Fragment 62

Rise up!

And become wakeful watchers

Of living men and corpses.

Fragment 63

Thunderbolt steers all things.

Fragment 64

Fire:

Want and satiety.

Fragment 65

Fire,

Having come suddenly upon them,

Will judge and convict all living beings.

Fragment 66

God is

Day and night, winter and summer;

War and peace, satiety and hunger;

And takes various shapes

Just as fire, mingled with perfumes,

Is named according to their scents.

Fragment 67

Soul

Heraclitus offers a good comparison of the soul to a spider and the body to a spider's web. Just as a spider, he says, waiting in the middle of the web, notices as soon as a fly damages its threads and quickly runs to the spot as if grieving over the wholeness of the thread, so man's soul, when any part of the body is harmed, quickly moves there as if troubled by the harm to the body to which it is firmly and proportionally connected.

Fragment 67a

Remedies

In the Wise, seeing and hearing of shameful things (phallic rites and obscene hymns) we are released from the harm caused by their corresponding deeds. And, therefore it was reasonable for Heraclitus to call these practices 'remedies.'

Fragment 68

Sacrifice

There are two kinds of sacrifices. The first are those of wholly purified men, such as may occur rarely in the case of a single man, as Heraclitus says, or a very small number. The other kind are immersed in matter, corporeal, and produced by change.

Fragment 69

Human opinions are but toys for children.

Fragment 70

Alas,

Man forgets where the way leads.

They are at odds with that

Which they most constantly associate

— The Reason which governs the Universe —

And what they meet with every day

Appears strange to them.

We should not act and speak

Like men asleep.

Fragments 71, 72, 73

We should not listen like children to their parents.

Fragment 74

Men asleep are also laborers and co-workers

In what takes place in the world.

Fragment 75

Death of fire is birth for air,

And the death of air is birth for water.

Fragment 76

It is delight,

Or death,

For souls to become moist.

Fragment 77

Human nature has no insight,

But the Divine has.

Fragment 78

A man is found foolish by a God,

As a child by a man.

Fragment 79

Know this:

War is common to all,

Strife is Justice,

And all things come to pass by Strife

And Necessity.

Fragment 80

Pythagoras:

Prince of imposters.

Fragment 81

The most beautiful of apes is ugly

In comparison with the race of man.

Fragment 82

The wisest of men seems an ape

Compared to a God.

Fragment 83

It rests by changing.

Fragment 84a

It is weariness to toil at the same task

And be always beginning.

Fragment 84b

It is hard to fight against the passions

For whatever it wants

It buys

At the price of Soul.

Fragment 85

The greater part of things Divine

Escape recognition

Because of disbelief and ignorance.

Fragment 86

A fool loves to get excited on any account.

Fragment 87

One and the same exists in us:

Living — Dead,

Waking — Sleeping,

Young — Old,

For these things having changed round are those,

And those things having changed round are these.

Fragment 88

The world of the Waking is one and shared

But the sleeping turn aside,

Each into a world of their own.

Fragment 89

All things are exchanged for Fire,

And Fire for all things,

As goods are for gold,

And gold for goods.

Fragment 90

One cannot step into the same river twice,

Nor can one grasp any mortal substance

in a stable condition,

It scatters and again gathers,

It forms and dissolves,

Approaches and departs.

Fragment 91

The Sibyl with raving lips

Utters solemn things,

Unadorned, unperfumed,

Her voice reaching over a thousand years

Because of the God speaking through her.

Fragment 92

The God whose Oracle is at Delphi

Neither declares,

Nor conceals,

But gives a sign.

Fragment 93

The Sun will not overstep his bounds,

For if He does,

The Erinyes, helpers of Justice,

Will find Him out.

Fragment 94

It is better to conceal our ignorance.

Fragment 95

We are now dead

And the body to us is a tomb.

Corpses should be thrown out faster than dung.

Fragment 96

Men,

Like dogs,

Also bark at those they do not recognize.

Fragment 97

Souls use the sense of smell in Hades.

Fragment 98

If there were no Sun

It would be night,

Despite the rest of the stars.

Fragment 99

Sun:

Overseer and Sentinel of cycles,

Determining changes and seasons

Which bring all things.

Fragment 100

I went in search of myself.

Fragment 101

Eyes are surer witnesses than ears.

Fragment 101a

To God all things are fair and just,

But men have supposed some things unjust

And some just.

Fragment 102

In a circle

Beginning

And end

Are one

And the same.

Fragment 103

For what sense or understanding do they have?

They believe the tales of poets

And take the crowd as their teachers,

Not knowing that most men are bad

And only few are good.

Fragment 104

Homer was an astronomer.

Fragment 105

Hesiod counted some days as good, others as bad,

Because he did not recognize that the nature of every day

Is the same.

Fragment 106

Eyes and ears are poor witnesses

If people have barbarous souls.

Fragment 107

Of all whose teachings I have heard,

None reaches this:

Recognizing how the Wise is

Different from any other thing.

Fragment 108

Fragment 109 = 95

It is not better for men to get all they want.

Fragment 110

It is disease that makes health pleasant and good,

Hunger satiety,

Weariness rest.

Fragment 111

Thinking soundly and Knowing the Self

Is the greatest excellence and wisdom:

Be watchful.

Act and speak Truth.

Perceive things according to their real nature.

Fragment 112

Understanding belongs to all.

Fragment 113

Those who will speak with understanding

Must hold fast to the Logos,

As a city holds fast to its law, and much more firmly.

For all human laws are nourished by Divine Law;

It extends as it will,

Suffices for all things,

And still surpasses.

Fragment 114

To the Soul belongs a Logos that transcends itself.

Fragment 115

The task is set to all men to know themselves

And to think soundly.

Fragment 116

A man when drunk

Stumbles,

And is led by a young boy,

Not knowing where he goes.

For his soul is wet.

Fragment 117

A dry soul is wisest and best;

It darts out of the body

Like lightning from a cloud.

Fragment 118

Man's character is his fate.

Fragment 119

The limits of evening and morning are the Bear,

And opposite the Bear,

The bounds of bright Zeus.

Fragment 120

The Ephesians would do well to hang themselves,

Every grown man of them,

And leave the city to young boys;

For they have banished Hermodorus,

The worthiest among them,

Saying:

'Let no one of us excel the rest;

Otherwise, be it elsewhere and among others.'

Fragment 121

Stepping near.

Fragment 122

Real nature loves to hide.

Fragment 123

The fairest world order

Is but a heap of random sweepings.

Fragment 124

The barley drink separates

If not stirred.

Fragment 125

May wealth never fail you, men of Ephesus,

So that you can be fully proved of being wicked.

Fragment 125a

Cold becomes warm, warm becomes cold;

Moist becomes dry, dry becomes wet.

Fragment 126

Pythagoras, son of Mnesarchus,

Practiced inquiry further than all other men, and,

Having made a selection,

Contrived a wisdom of his own:

Barren learning,

Base deceit.

Fragment 129

There is a certain order and fixed time

For the changes of the world

In accordance with some destined Necessity.

Fragment A5

The Great Year

There is also a year, whose winter is a great flood and whose summer is a world conflagration. In these alternating periods the world is now going up in flames, now turning to water. This cycle, according to Heraclitus, consists of 10,800 solar years.

Fragment A13

The Soul is an exhalation that perceives;

Different from the body,

Always flowing.

Fragment A15

A generation, according to Heraclitus, is thirty years, the length of time from the begetting of a grandfather till that of his grandson.

Fragment A19

Homer was wrong when he said:

'Would that strife might vanish

From among Gods and men.'

For there is no harmony without high and low notes,

Nor any animal without male and female,

Both of which are opposites.

Fragment A22

In taking the poets as testimony for things unknown,

They are citing authorities that are untrustworthy.

Fragment A23

Our soul is a spark of stellar essence.

Fragment without DK number

Ω

Ω

A Note about the Logos

In the Introduction we quoted Marcus Aurelius who wrote in his notebook, to remind himself daily of the following words of Heraclitus:

... and that men quarrel with that with which they are most constantly in communion, the Reason which governs the universe...

"The Reason which governs the universe" is how Marcus Aurelius understood Heraclitus' logos, as a cosmic ordering principle.

In Plutarch we find the following passage:

Philosophy embraces inquiry, wonder, and doubt, it seems natural that most of the things relating to the God should have been hidden away in riddles, and should require some account of their purpose, and an explanation of the cause. (Plutarch, *De E apud Delphous*, II).

The logos can be seen as "the things related to the God" as well as their explanation—both.

Entire books and countless scholarly articles have been written about the logos of Heraclitus and how to interpret this rich word in his fragments. In ancient Greece the word logos already had a number of meanings, expanding over time: from spoken word, discourse, account, measure, to law, reason, principle, formula, teaching, etc. It has a root-sense of being something uttered that conveys, explains, and uncovers and has retained that meaning. In the Book of John:

In the beginning was the Word (Logos), and the Word was with God, and the Word was God.
(John.1)

Logos has the meaning of "cosmic utterance," or "the eternal Word" as it was used by Heraclitus, especially when we look at the fragments in their totality, as a whole system or teaching. Heraclitus demonstrates in the shortest of sentences an entire model of the cosmos, and in it he places man, his soul and their reason for being. What governs this model is an unassailable intelligence, a divine, continuous presence, that pervades everything. That is the logos of Heraclitus. Later philosophers sometimes called that the "Divine Logos."

A modern description of Heraclitus' logos, from scholar Enrique Hülsz:

"A continuous presence, perceived but unrecognized by most men."

Bruno Snell, in *The Discovery of the Mind* writes:

Heraclitus turns off in a completely new direction. On the one hand he interprets the divine substance more abstractly as Mind, and on the other he points to this as the ultimate goal of human knowledge. All experience, necessary as it is, remains without value unless it leads to an intensive understanding of the logos, the fundament of which speech is only the superstructure, and whose objective existence is implied in every word that hits the mark...

He partakes of divine knowledge, that his comprehension of the role of the deity in the world transcends the opinions held by the mass of the people.

This divine element anchored in the depth of the soul. (Snell, pages 144-145).

The Stoics often used the term "Divine Reason" in place of "logos" and so demonstrate their understanding of the meaning Heraclitus already infused in his use of the term.

Such an understanding makes sense, especially in view of other fragments, particularly Fragments 50 and 114 where the Logos can be seen as that divine and continuous presence that can flow through one (see, Fragment 50: It is wise then for those who are listening, not to me, but to the Logos, to agree that all things are one; Fragment 114: Those who will speak with understanding must hold fast to the Logos).

It also makes sense in terms of practically applying Heraclitus' fragments to our life today. A dogmatic reading of logos *only* as "speech", "account" or "discourse" and worse, refusing the possibility that more than that was meant, is an alternative but then serves to close off a deeper understanding of this living teaching. Important as well is to not get stuck in the trap of clinging to our own or others' opinions about what Logos "should" mean (see, Fragment 28a: The most esteemed man holds fast to just imaginings).

The objection by some scholars to an interpretation of the word logos in a more "cosmic" sense, as expressing eternal truth and reality, with terms such as "the Word", "Divine Truth", "Divine Reason," "the Way of management of the All" or "the Reason which governs the universe" as Marcus Aurelius did, is that such use imposes an anachronistic gloss, a meaning which was not there at the time of Heraclitus and therefore could not have been his.

That argument underestimates the tremendous new influence of what took place in the sixth century BCE. It had already started before Heraclitus but he broke new ground. In this period where an entire civilization was being conceived by a handful of men, initial changes were monumental, but also of an almost invisible nature that can defy observation.

Heraclitus was the first to describe the soul as having depth (Fragment 45: You will not find out the limits of the soul by going, even if you travel over every way, so deep is its logos). He was also the first to describe the soul as having a logos that increases itself (Fragment 115). The concept of "eternal truth" as connected to logos was already current in Ionic Greek.

Burnet notes in relation to Fragment 1:

The logos is primarily the discourse of Heraclitus himself; though as he is a prophet, we may call it his 'Word.' (Early Greek Philosophy, page 133, footnote 1).

Wheelwright in *Heraclitus*, Chapter 1, points out that Epicharmus, a near-contemporary of Heraclitus, also wrote about a divine Logos:

The Logos steers men and ever preserves them in the right way. Man has the power of calculation, but there is also the divine Logos. Human reasoning is sprung from the divine Logos, which furnishes to each man the passageway of both life and nourishment. (Epicharmus, Fragment 57).

Werner Jaeger, a tremendously insightful classicist, writes:

Logos for Heraclitus was not conceptual thinking. It was a form of knowledge, the origin of both 'action and speech.' If we want an example of this special type of knowledge, we shall not find it in thought, which teaches that what is can never not be, but in the insight which struck out such a brilliant truth as 'Ethos is a man's daemon.' [Fragment 119].

It is highly important and significant that in the very first sentence of his book (a sentence which is fortunately preserved) Heraclitus lays down that knowledge has a productive relation to life. There he speaks of the words and actions that men attempt without grasping the logos which alone teaches them to 'do while awake' those actions which those without it do 'while asleep.' That is, logos can give a new life of conscious knowledge.

The prophetic tone of his speech derived its logical power and urgency from his claim as a philosopher to open men's eyes to their own actions, to reveal to the the foundations of life, to awaken them from sleep.

Even the logos cannot be defined except in metaphor.
(From Jaeger's *Paideia*, Volume I, at pages 180-181, footnotes omitted).

In *The Theology of the Early Greek Philosophers*, at page 112, Jaeger adds:

The beginning of the work tells of the 'word' that the Philosopher proclaims—the logos. Men fail to understand it even though it is eternal. They understand it neither before they hear it nor when they have heard it first. But even if this 'logos' is primarily the word of Heraclitus himself, it is not merely his word as a man among men, but one that expresses eternal truth and reality and is therefore itself eternal...

This is not the language of a teacher and scholar, but that of a prophet intent on rousing men from their slumber.

The endless argument in scholarly circles about the meaning of the term logos, whether or not there is a "doctrine of the logos" to be found in Heraclitus, and if it is even acceptable to write Logos with a capital L, is in itself ironic as this is exactly what Heraclitus predicts in this first fragment: man will forever fail to understand the logos. Like the sleepers we are, we turn to our own private understanding.

Peter Kingsley writes:

Modern interpretations and translations of logos as used before Plato's time are still grotesquely over-rationalized. (*Reality*, page 566).

Finkelberg recently (2017) brought a fresh perspective on the question of the logos and points out that from the very first sentence we can see the opposite of the logos at work: living as though we have a private understanding.

> [This]...*renders the logos synonymous with understanding, which, as the Anonymous Source reports, is 'an explanation of the way of management of the All.'*
>
> *Since the agent of the management of the All is the logos managing all things (fragment 72), the logos stands for both the agent of the management of all things and the knowledge how all things are managed and, since all things are the One, also of their unity: Having listened not to me to but to the logos, it is wise to agree that all things are one (thing)' (Fragment 50).* (Finkelberg, Heraclitus and Thales' Conceptual Scheme, page 189).

Also in relation to Heraclitus' first fragment, Finkelberg writes that the reference to those who have heard the logos for the first time implies that there may be a recurrent hearing of the logos that brings about a greater awareness, it is "perceiver-dependent," and as a result of this:

> *It follows that one's hearing of the logos must be complemented by laborious efforts to grasp the ways of divine agency in the world.* (pages 200-201).

This brings us then hopefully a step closer to a productive understanding of the term logos, because just as in the river-simile (Fragments 12 and 91), we cannot hear the logos twice in the same way: once we have changed, meaning, once we have increased our ability to hear its message, we will understand Heraclitus' logos in deeper and deeper ways.

I will tell you that the soul knows the eternal Word better than any philosopher can describe it. (Meister Eckhart).

Ω

Sources, Context, Notes on Fragments

For each fragment we list the ancient source where the text can be found. Where helpful (hopefully) we provide some context, quotes or commentary.

Fragment 1

From Sextus Empiricus, *Adversus Mathematicos*, VII, 1, 32.

There is general agreement that Fragment 1 was the start of Heraclitus' book. Beyond that, we are not sure of the order the fragments were in.

Bywater translates logos in this fragment as "Universal Reason." We can also think of it as Divine Truth in this context.

The "words and works" are a common reference in Heraclitus' time to the sum total of a man's life: one's words —his thoughts—and his works—his deeds or actions.

Knowledge for Heraclitus implies both speech and action.

Fragment 2

From Sextus Empiricus, *Adversus Mathematicos*, VII, 1, 33.

This fragment is echoed in Fragment 89: The world of the waking is one and shared but the sleeping turn aside each into a world of their own. Heraclitus exhorts us to folllow the Logos (Divine Reason), not our own thinking.

Another echo of this fragment is found in Cleanthes' *Hymn to Zeus* where we find the following lines:

That of the Whole a single Scheme (Logos) arises everlasting, which men neglect and overlook, as many are evil;

Another translation of Fragment 2 is: "Although the *logos* is common, the many live as if they have a private understanding." See, e.g., Long, *Hellenistic Philosophy*, page 145.

The word "common" or "shared" as it is sometimes translated, should be understood in the sense of "universal" or "pervading everything" in that the living *logos* rules all, pertains to all, and there is only one truth for all, but as Heraclitus already declared in Fragment 1, most of us are currently oblivious and do not understand the logos. Therefore the meaning of "common" in the sense that all people know or understand it would not be correct.

In the same sense as "common," Heraclitus says that knowing ourselves and thinking soundly is our birthright, in Fragment 116 (It belongs to all men to know themselves and to think soundly). But as this is the greatest excellence (Fragment 112—Thinking soundly is the greatest excellence and wisdom…), it can only be accomplished by that war, that inner strife mentioned in Fragment 8 (All things come to pass through strife), and in Fragment 80 (War is common to all, strife is justice, and all things come to pass by strife and necessity).

Heraclitus and T.S. Eliot's Four Quartets

Fragments 2 and 60 (The way up and the way down are one and the same) are epigraphs (short, stand-alone quotes) at the start of *Burnt Norton*, the first poem of the work *The Four Quartets* by T.S. Eliot:

τοῦ λόγου δὲ ἐόντος ξυνοῦ ζώουσιν οἱ πολλοί ὡς ἰδίαν ἔχοντες φρόνησιν [I. p. 77. Fr. 2.]

ὁδὸς ἄνω κάτω μία καὶ ωὐτή [I. p. 89. Fr. 60.]

Diels: Die Fragmente der Vorsokratiker (Herakleitos).

Eliot left these quotations in their original Greek because he felt that he could not do them justice in a translation. About the Logos he had previously written that *"...to the Greek there was something inexplicable about the Logos so that it was a participation of man with the divine.*

Throughout the entire *Four Quartets* Eliot infuses his words with beautiful direct and indirect references and understanding from Heraclitus' fragments. Eliot describes the highest mystical experiences Eliot himself had—*moments out of time*—as well as his thoughts about time, eternity, man in relation to the universe and the elements of water, earth, air and fire, so prominent in Heraclitus' Fragments. Thus we read in Eliot's masterwork the following (and so much more):

Time present and time past
Are both perhaps present in time future
And time future contained in time past.
If all time is eternally present
All time is unredeemable.

...

What might have been and what has been
Point to one end which is always present.

...

Time past and time future
Allow but a little consciousness.
To be conscious is not to be in time.
But only in time can the moment in the rose-garden,
The moment in the arbour where the rain beat,
The moment in the draughty church at smokefall
Be remembered; involved with past and future.
Only through time time is conquered.

...

In my beginning is my end.

I sometimes wonder if that is what Krishna meant—
Among other things—or one way of putting the same thing;
That the future is a faded song, a Royal Rose or a lavender spray
Of whistful regret for those who are not yet here to regret,
Pressed between yellow leaves of a book that has never been opened.
And the way up is the way down, the way forward is the way back.
   …

   Fare forward travellers! not escaping from the past
   Into different lives, or into any future;
   You are not the same people who left that station
   Or who will arrive at any terminus
   …
   Men's curiosity searches past and future
   And clings to that dimension. But to apprehend
   The point of intersection of the timeless
   With time, is an occupation for the saint—
   No occupation either, but something given
   And taken, in a lifetime's death in love,
   Ardour and selflessness and self-surrender,
   For most of us, there is only the unattended
   Moment, the moment in and out of time.
   …
   Water and fire succeed
   The town, the pasture and the weed,
   Water and fire deride
   The sacrifice that we denied.
   Water and fire shall rot
   The marred foundations we forgot,
   Of sanctuary and choir.
   This is the death of water and fire.

Fragment 3

From Aetius, II, 21.

This fragment is often understood by commentators as saying that the sun is simply the size it appears to be.

Schönbeck points out that what this fragment and Fragments 94 and 120 have in common is that the sun is presented as "having a metrical capacity at his disposal and as suitable for being limited in a regulatory manner":

> *That something like 'size' exists, seems obvious. Insofar as standard norms may come to mind here, the matter is not clear from the outset, certainly considering the difference in culture between Ionia in about 500 B.C. and Western civilizations 25 centuries later. Anaxagoras posed that the sun is many times larger than the Peleponnessos.* (From: Sunbowl or Symbol, page 206).

Fragment 4

From Albertus Magnus, *de vegetab.* VI, 401.

Heraclitus said that if happiness consisted in the pleasures of the body, we should call oxen happy whenever they find bitter vetch to eat.

Fragment 5

From *Theosophia*, 68 and Origen, *Contra Celsum*, VII, 62.

Fragment 6

From Aristotle, *Meteorologica*, Book 2, p. 354.

From: Plato's *Republic VI:*

> *The question how the study of philosophy may be so ordered as not to be the ruin of the State: All great attempts are*

attended with risk; 'hard is the good' as men say. Still, he said, let the point be cleared up, and the enquiry will then be complete.

I shall not be hindered, I said, by any want of will, but, if at all, by a want of power: my zeal you may see for yourselves; and please to remark in what I am about to say how boldly and unhesitatingly I declare that States should pursue philosophy, not as they do now, but in a different spirit.

In what manner?

At present, I said, the students of philosophy are quite young; beginning when they are hardly past childhood, they devote only the time saved from moneymaking and housekeeping to such pursuits; and even those of them who are reputed to have most of the philosophic spirit, when they come within sight of the great difficulty of the subject, I mean dialectic, take themselves off. In after life when invited by some one else, they may, perhaps, go and hear a lecture, and about this they make much ado, for philosophy is not considered by them to be their proper business: at last, when they grow old, in most cases they are extinguished more truly than Heracleitus' sun, inasmuch as they never light up again.

(Translation by Benjamin Jowett).

Fragment 7

From Aristotle, *De Sensu*, 5, 443.

The senses are the paths for impressions of the world to us. Smell is a more limited sense than the chief senses of sight and hearing, which in Fragment 55 Heraclitus says he prefers (Fragment 55: Whatever comes from sight, hearing, learning from experience: this I prefer).

But even those senses are untrustworthy, as he states in Fragment 46 (Seeing is being deceived) and Fragment 107 (But eyes and ears are poor witnesses if people have barbarous souls).

Smell is the only sense left to us in sleep. In Fragment 98 Heraclitus says the souls use the sense of smell in Hades (the underworld).

Fragment 8

From: Aristotle, *Nicomachean Ethics*, VIII, 1.

Kahn explains the figurative sense of the terms convergent and divergent: *"the hindrance is a benefit"* and *"opposition is profitable."*

Fragment 9

From: Aristotle, *Nicomachean Ethics* X, 5.

Instead of garbage we can read "chaff," the normal food for donkeys. Or substitute "fiat" as in: Asses prefer fiat over bitcoin. IYKYK.

Fragment 10

From: Aristotle, *De Mundo* 5, 396.

Fragment 11

From: Aristotle, *De Mundo* 6:

> Both wild and domestic animals, and those living upon land or in air or water, are born and die in conformity with the laws of God. For every beast, as Heraclitus says, "is driven by blows."

The blows are the strokes of the thunderbolt; the Gods guiding mankind. Marcovich, page 430.

Plato: *The Gods drive us as a shepherd his flocks.* (From *Critias*, 109).

Fragment 12

From Arius Didymus, fragment 39, 2.

Man in relation to eternity by piercing time. This is one of Heraclitus' most famous sayings and has been stated as "everything changes", Panta rhei (Greek: πάντα ῥεῖ), and has been called "Heraclitus' law of absolute instability" and the "principle of flux." Seneca quotes the fragment as follows:

> *Into the same rivers we step and do not step;*
>
> *We are and we are not.*

Dilcher observes:

These fragments are not meant to formulate a theory concerning single physical objects, to the effect that there is literally no rest in the ubiquitous flux of things, and that all apparent standstill is an illusion.

Heraclitus does not deny that certain things temporarily come to a halt and stop moving and changing. What he is concerned with is to point at the necessity of constant change in a living being in order to keep being alive. Only at death it comes to a rest. When alive, it will incessantly transform, not in order to change its appearance, but on the contrary simply to maintain itself. Thus it rests by changing. (Dilcher, page 94–footnote omitted).

The sameness of the river is maintained by the flow of water. ... Likewise, the logos which explicates this structure consists in this moving dialectical process of understanding. (Dilcher, page 114).

From Plato, *Symposium*, page 207:

'Marvel not,' she said, 'if you believe that love is of the immortal, as we have several times acknowledged; for here again, and on the same principle too, the mortal nature is seeking as far as is possible to be everlasting and immortal: and this is only to be attained by generation, because generation always leaves behind a new existence in the place of the old.

Nay even in the life of the same individual there is succession and not absolute unity: a man is called the same, and yet in the short interval which elapses between youth and age, and in which every animal is said to have life and identity, he is undergoing a perpetual process of loss and reparation—hair, flesh, bones, blood, and the whole body are always changing.

Which is true not only of the body, but also of the soul, whose habits, tempers, opinions, desires, pleasures, pains, fears, never remain the same in any one of us, but are always coming and going; and equally true of knowledge, and what is still more surprising to us mortals, not only do the sciences in general spring up and decay, so that in respect of them we are never the same; but each of them individually experiences a like change.

(Translated by Benjamin Jowett).

Fragment 13

From Clement, *Stromateis* I, 2, 2.

Fragment 14

From Clement, *Protrepticus*, 22, 2.

Fragment 15

From Clement, *Protrepticus*, 34, 5.

Fragment 16

Clement, *Paedagogus*, II, 99, 5.

A reference to the all-seeing, ever-awake Zeus.

Fragment 17

From Clement, *Stromateis*, II, 8, 1.

Fragment 18

From Clement, *Stromateis*, II, 17, 4.

This fragment is often glossed over, likely because we have heard the saying "expect the unexpected" so often that we are no longer surprised by its advice. But scholar Andrew Mason proposes that "expecting the unexpected" could be *transitive*: causing something to happen to what is otherwise inaccessible and undiscoverable that would not be possible without it. (See, *Heraclitus' Usage of ὅστις in Fragments DK B 5 and B 27*, at page 63, and see Fragment 27: What men awaits at death…).

Omen-Mindedness : Expect a Sign

Heraclitus tells us that without an effort of preparation on our part, the "expecting," we will not find what we need to find: the "unexpected." The way to it is unexplored. Because we do not prepare by "expecting" (whatever that work of preparation entails) we will always miss it, not see it for what it is, or perhaps be surprised and thrown off balance by it. What is at stake is that once we come face-to-face with the unexpected we are supposed to be finding, we are not ready for it, we don't recognize what we have just touched upon and the moment has passed us by. Different and again different waters will have past us by.

One of the tools the Greeks used was the mindset of being "omen-minded." This is something we can consider adopting, because it can be a form of preparation along the lines of the psychological approach outlined by Mason. In other words, the preparation itself—the work of becoming omen-minded—will change our coming into contact with the unexpected in a subtle but important way.

This is not a suggestion we read about very often! Mostly, what is taken away from this fragment is a vague sense that we need more diligence, more hard work. In short, we continue to look for something outside of ourself. Omen-mindedness involves not just looking for signs and omens outside of ourselves but also a looking within because we need to create a receptive space in ourselves. Thus, through our attention, we create a connection between ourselves and with what is outside ourselves. Maintaining that connection is a kind of tension or strife: a bow is being flexed.

For more about the Greek use of signs and omens, see Bibliography and Further Reading, under Beerden, Dillon, and Flower.

Kim Beerden, in *Worlds Full of Signs: Ancient Greek Divination in Context*, writes:

> *Divination was omnipresent in the ancient world: "If the ancient Mediterranean world was full of gods it was full of their messages as well." The mindset of ancient individuals might even be described as a state of "omen-mindedness," as is testified by the amount and nature of the ancient evidence.* (page 9).

> *The occurrence of spontaneous signs was based on an existing reciprocal relationship between the humans and the supernatural. The supernatural was thought to provide a sign voluntarily and because it wanted to. Everyone enjoyed such a reciprocal relationship with the supernatural: this includes women, slaves and children of all ages.*

The individual had already established a relationship with the supernatural by giving a gift beforehand, or was going to do so at some point in the future. The preexistence of these relationships means that everyone could receive a spontaneous sign without giving the supernatural a particular gift in exchange for the sign. (page 111– footnotes omitted).

Being omen-minded can be seen as a state of approaching ourselves, our life and all things in it as getting us ready and open to occurrences and events possibly signifying something to us, showing a direction to us (on this trackless Way). Rather than initially focusing on where these signs or messages comes from and what they could mean, let's turn to what is happening on our end.

With the practice of being omen-minded there is a certain flexing of alertness and readiness: we have to be on the lookout for signs, otherwise we miss most, if not all of them. Being watchful is already a giant step up from oblivion. This is the gift we are giving beforehand. "Be watchful and strenghten the things that remain..." it is written in the biblical book of Revelation 3:2.

Being on the lookout and taking note of signs, even when there is no sign, or if we are not sure there is a sign, or if there is no immediate or obvious meaning in the sign to be discerned is in itself of incalculable benefit, *and probably even more so*, because we train our awareness, and by doing so make our senses and soul more receptive to subtle influences, changes, ideas and we can start to see better the "real nature of things."

Importantly, we can and should always use any sign we observe (or think we observe) to remind ourself to begin again being on the lookout. In so doing, the omen-mindedness sustains itself. An increase in our awareness is ultimately our goal and that's the reason it doesn't matter if the sign "really was a sign" or not. As there is no "proving" of a sign, it will often only have meaning for the person using the sign.

A sign can be something out of the ordinary, but also something quite ordinary and common, such as something said or done by a child or an animal, or our eye falling on something we were just meant to read. In the beginning of this process we may well find ourself without experience (see, Fragment 1).

Beerden says:

The first element in the divinatory process is a sign: "[...] anything, whether object, sound, action, or event, which is capable of standing for something in some respect. A divinatory sign had to be recognized. It could be something which an individual observed and recognized as being significant: a sign could therefore be a special occurrence, a disruption in the pattern of normality. However, a sign could also be something perfectly normal which only became significant at the moment at which an individual observed it and recognized it as a sign. (Beerden, page 22).

While the sign is perceived through our senses, the first step has to be our open attentiveness coming from within. We are now on the lookout and more able to recognize. While some signs can temporarily startle us from our oblivion, we will be far more aware of and receptive to a multitude of less obvious signs.

Before we move on to what signs could mean and actions to take, let's pause here and quote from Bruno Snell's *The Discovery of the Mind* where the new direction in the history of philosophy and thought Heraclitus took is described very well. It very much relates to the depth of this work of attention and explains how Heraclitus had such an impact on science, as this is the foundation of reasoning by analogy. To distill this thread, we will take sentences and parts of sentences in a different order than they are found in the book:

This delight in a wealth of experience [enthusiasm for investigation as a basis for theory, i.e., conjecture] *which was so prominent in archaic Greece, and which was not to be extinguished until the days of the classical period, met its first adversary in the person of Heraclitus, with whose pronouncement concerning the ignorance of humankind we opened this chapter: Much learning (polymathie) does not teach anyone to have intelligence (noos).*

Heraclitus rejects the very thing which had become the prime object of human inquiry. In place of extensive searching he demands an intensive approach: Wisdom is one thing: to understand the intelligence which steers all through all things.

[Heraclitus'] investigation does not dissipate itself in different directions. All experience, necessary as it is, remains without value unless it leads to an intensive understanding of the logos. The exploration of Heraclitus does not contend itself with the course of experience, the road which leads to the external world. He says: 'I searched into myself.'

Men are not awake, he says, they resemble those who are in deep sleep or they may be likened to the drunken; they are like children or like the beasts, a charge which recurs time after time. Heraclitus also wants to penetrate to an invisible core, to a reality which needs to be uncovered. For the understanding of this logos he does not propose a mystic communion, nor does he demonstrate a methodical approach, although in his thought too the visible signs are a means of attaining the invisible.

He urges man to be watchful, and to pay heed to what nature has to say. In as much as the logos pervades everything, it manifests itself in the individual also; and yet is set apart from all things since it transcends the particular.

*The mysterious essence, the **vital tension, reveals itself through significant particular events which man uses as symbols to apprehend the divine.** For Heraclitus they are **symbols in which the wise man catches a glimpse of the profound secrets of life.***

Heraclitus shows us the meaning of the 'necessary' metaphor. The truth Heraclitus has set himself to unveil cannot be expressed in any other way than an image. We realize that the truth it expresses lies far below the level of human or animal activity, that it is one with the very roots of our existence. This is the life that cannot be grasped intellectually.

*It **appears to us in the most diverse forms** in which it is always complete; and **these forms, in turn, are the only channels through which life may establish contact with man. They are its only means of achieving expression**.* (Snell, pages 17, 146-149, 218-222, fragment numbers omitted, emphasis added).

Once we start being more alert to signs, there will be times when we wonder what a particular sign could mean and what action to take. About the interpretation of oracles (and this applies to signs as well), Flower writes in *The Seer in Ancient Greece*:

When the Pythia so wished, she was capable of giving explicit advice in plain language. But when she was dealing with a particularly difficult or delicate problem, she composed verse responses in which were embedded a variety of possible recommendations and a range of possible consequences.

For ambiguity is not necessarily evasive. Rather, oracular ambiguity served to define the limits of the problem and the range of possible solutions, and then to refer the problem back to the inquirer. The inquirer, through the act of interpretation, then provided his own answer. But it must be stressed that this answer was not the only possible answer, because many such oracles were open to being interpreted in different ways. (pages 234-235).

One useful way dealing with the questions and ambiguity at this stage is to continue to "look within", as Marcus Aurelius exhorts us, and continue with being "in search of ourself" (as Heraclitus says in Fragment 101). That way we can live the question itself and observe it and our responses to it.

There is a trap in that a lot of what we see, feel, think and believe about signs is just our "imaginings" we should let go of, (Fragment 28a), or that we do not recognize yet what we are experiencing (Fragment 17). There is the weariness of always being a beginner (Fragment 84: It is weariness to toil at the same task and be always beginning). Another trap is, of course, our own arrogance about our ability to interpret signs, our importance receiving such signs, etc. This hubris should be doused faster than a raging fire (Fragment 43).

A few additional Stoic principles that can be useful in this regard, and that go hand-in-hand are evenness or even-temperedness, leading to non-judgment; and acceptance, allowing appreciation of the Divine in all things, even the smallest.

In *Forgotten Stoic: Plotinus—Strain and See*, we note that a common trap of judgment can be for us to focus on outward manifestations and ascribe lower motivations to another's (Stoic) actions, such as seeing indifference (or worse) where even-temperedness is attempted, practiced or demonstrated. We should aim to be non-judgmental and cleanse or purify our observing faculty (*Strain and See*) on our way to moulding our character (a large part of which is letting go of what is not of our highest nature).

The medieval German mystic Meister Eckhart (1260-1328) speaks to us about that discipline of evenness in the following fragment, called "Envoi" and it directly goes to the heart of the inner practice of preparing our ruling faculty to receive signs of a higher world, here called God. As Eckhart elsewhere said: *The heart is not made pure by prayer as a physical act, but rather the prayer is made pure by the pure heart.*

Envoi

Meister Eckhart's good friends bade him: "Since you are going to leave us, give us one last word."

"I will give you," he replied, "a rule which is the stronghold of all I have ever said, in which are lodged all the truths to be discussed or put into practice."

It often happens that what seems trivial to us is more important to God than what we think important. Therefore, we ought to take everything God puts on us evenly, not comparing and wondering which is more important, or higher or best. We ought simply to follow where God leads, that is, to do what we are most inclined to do, to go where we are repeatedly admonished to go—to where we feel most drawn. If we do that, God gives us his greatest in our least and never fails.

Now, some people despise the little things of life. It is their mistake, for they thus prevent themselves from getting God's greatness out of these little things. God is every way, evenly in all ways, to him who has the eyes to see. But sometimes it is hard to know whether one's inclinations come from God or not, but that can be decided this way: If you find yourself always possessed of a knowledge or intimation of God's will, which you obey before everything else, because you feel urged to obey it and the urge is frequent, then you may know that it is from God.

Some people want to recognize God only in some pleasant enlightenment—and then they get pleasure and enlightenment but not God. Somewhere it is written that God shines in the darkness where every now and then we get a glimpse of him. More often, God is where his light is

least apparent. Therefore we ought to expect God in all manners and all things evenly.

Someone may now say: I should be glad to look for God evenly in all shapes and things, but my mind does not always work the same way—and then, not as well with this as with that. To which I reply: That is too bad! All paths lead to God and he is on them all evenly, to him who knows. I am well aware that a person may get more out of one technique than another but it is not best so. God responds to all techniques evenly to a knowing man. Such and such may be the way, but it is not God.

But even if God is in all ways and all things evenly, do I not still need a special way to get to him? Let us see. Whatever the way that leads you most frequently to awareness of God, follow that way; and if another way appears, different from the first, and you quit the first and take the second, and the second works, it is all right.

It would be nobler and better, however, to achieve rest and security through evenness, by which one might take God and enjoy him in any manner, in any thing, and not have to delay and hunt around for your special way: *that has been my joy!* To this end all kinds of activities may contribute and any work may be a help; but if it does not, let it go!

From: *Meister Eckhart, A Modern Translation*; Fragment 44. Translation by Raymond Bernard Blackney; pp. 249-250. Emphasis added.

Fragment 19

From Clement, *Stromateis*, II, 24, 5.

Fragment 20

From Clement, *Stromateis* III, 14, 1.

Fragment 21

From Clement, *Stromateis* III, 21, 1.

Fragment 22

From Clement, *Stromateis* IV, 4, 2.

Fragment 23

From Clement, *Stromateis* IV, 9, 7.

Fragment 24

From Clement, *Stromateis* IV, 16, 1.

Fragment 25

From Clement, *Stromateis* IV, 49, 2.

Fragment 26

From Clement, *Stromateis* IV, 141, 2.

A Man is Kindled as a Light in the Night

Context from Clement:

> *Whatever they say of sleep, the same must be understood of death, for it is plain that each of them is a departure from life, the one less, the other more. Which is also to be received from Heraclitus: Man is kindled as a light at night; in like manner, dying, he is extinguished...*

The first line of this fragment is often translated as "A man kindles a light for himself..."

To be kindled as a light in the night, rather than kindling a light for oneself, evokes the idea of man being touched by a higher influence, a conscious source, rather than doing it alone and without help.

One of the most remarkable and strange things about man's oblivion, his being asleep, is that the fact this state has to be pointed out to us.

We actually have to be shown we are asleep, veiled, and a first unveiling is akin to being touched, being kindled by a watcher. This is something that we cannot "do" on our own, for ourselves. There has to be a reaching out from both sides and it means sacrifice.

See also Leon Ruiz, pages 104-109 *The Man of Light* for a beautiful understanding of this fragment as a description of enlightenment.

A short excerpt:

> ...*we can read his words here as self-referential. Heraclitus is presenting himself to us as the man of light who is able to lead a person out of the blindness of the night of ignorance into the light of true understanding, that is, ultimately, self-knowledge—the return of oneself to oneself, the end of the bitter estrangement from and ignorance of one's true nature.*

> *We are being shown the nature of the spiritual work talked about above. A watcher or a guardian does not merely sit by as an objective, detached observer. To truly keep watch over people, to guard them, is to be a guide. The watcher leads the blind by the hand.*

> *He presents them with their own immortal natures for the first time.* (Leon Ruiz, page 109).

Fragment 27

From Clement, *Stromateis* IV, 144, 3.

This fragment is like a drawing with an optical illusion, where we have to gaze, squint or change focus to see a hidden message or to see a double meaning in it.

Commonly, this fragment is translated as:

What awaits men at death they cannot expect or even imagine.

We now have the fragment as follows, following the analysis in an insightful 2014 article by scholar Andrew J. Mason:

There await men when they die whichever things they do not expect for themselves or even imagine.

The second reading, equally supported by the words and wording of the fragment, does not restrict this to just our first impression that man is mistaken about what happens after death. In the second reading Mason points out:

On this construal B27 does not assert, while remaining silent about them, that there are certain things that await all of us in common when we die. Nor does it restrict the object of men's expectations to the afterlife. What it is really talking about is the living: not just what they expect but the way they expect and go about their lives in expectation.

Life, it seems, is in an essential sense about learning how to expect properly, and what we do not learn in life we will have to come to terms with after death. Heraclitus even seems to give a clue to what this involves: not expecting for oneself, from a narrowly personal and self-interested standpoint. (Mason, page 59).

About Heraclitus' style, Mason says in connection with these two readings, that *the very straightforwardness* [of reading 1] *counts against it.*

It is not his way to hand to hand things to us on a platter, nor to contend himself with truisms. Heraclitus proclaims himself the bearer of a truth never before attained…

At the same time, and indeed for just this reason, he has the option of seeming to advert to the truisms of folk wisdom while quietly introducing a twist which changes everything, if only it is caught sight of. (Mason, page 60).

Fragment 28a
From Clement, *Stromateis* V, 9, 3.

Fragment 28b
From Clement, *Stromateis* V, 9, 3.

Fragment 29
From Clement, *Stromateis* V, 59, 4.

Choose the One Thing

Choosing the one thing means to do one thing well: give priority to the inner work Heraclitus outlines—trying his "words and works" on the path in search of ourselves— and this above all else.

The exchange is literally the payment we have to make to get to know ourself, to "think soundly" and it means letting go of our hubris, opinions, disbelief, ignorance, illusions, imaginings, and sleep.

We need to tame our animal desires and indulgences (such as gluttony in this fragment), as well as our passions, so we can think and act what is true and start learning to perceive things according to their real nature, seeing the unity in all things.

Heraclitus is absolutely uncompromising.

This fragment echoes Thales, who said:

> *Many words do not declare an understanding heart. Seek one sole wisdom. Choose one sole good. For thou wilt check the tongues of pratterers without end.*

Meister Eckhart also keeps it simple:

> *Perfection depends **only** on accepting poverty, misery, hardship, disappointment, and whatever comes in course, and accepting it willingly, gladly, freely, eagerly until death, **as if one were prepared for it [the expecting]** and therefore unmoved by it and not asking why.*

And in the following excerpts from Eckhart's fragments, about choosing that one sole good:

> *If a man goes seeking God and, with God, something else, he will not find God; but if one seeks only God—and really so—he will never find only God but along with God himself he will find all that God is capable of. If you seek your own advantage or blessings through God you are not really seeking God at all.*

> *When one puts something before God, he makes God nothing, and nothing, God.*

> *When I pray for something, I do not pray; when I pray for nothing, I really pray.*

> *To pray for anything except God might be called idolatry or injustice.*

> *Any object you have on your mind, however good, with be a barrier between you and the inmost truth.*

> *There never was a struggle or a battle which required greater valor that that in which a man forgets or denies himself.*

Fragment 30

From Clement, *Stromateis* V, 103.

From Jaeger's *Paideia*, Vol. I, page 184 (footnote omitted).

[Heraclitus] *taught that through its kinship with the 'everliving fire' of the cosmos the philosophical soul is capable of knowing divine wisdom and harboring it in itself.*

Thus the conflict between the cosmology and the religion of the sixth century was resolved into unity in Heraclitus, who stood at the threshold of the new century. We have already observed that the cosmos of the Milesians was rather a universal moral code than a law of nature in the modern sense. Heraclitus raised its moral character to a cosmic religion, in his 'divine nomos', and thus based the moral code of the philosophical man upon the moral law of the entire universe.

Fragment 31a and 31b

From Clement, *Stromateis* V, 104.

Translated here as "fiery wind such as forms the stars" (a translation from Shuster) is the word "prēstēr" which as Kahn (who translates as "lightning storm") points out emphasizes a connection with fire from heaven in ancient Greek literary evidence:

"The word first appears in Hesiod's Theogony as an attribute of winds...as an instance of celestial flame." ...

"On any reasonable interpretation, a prēstēr is not an element or a cosmic mass, but a devastating discharge of fire as a visual experience." (Kahn, page 142).

Fragment 32

From Clement, *Stromateis* V, 115, 1.

Osho, in his lectures on Heraclitus in 1974, said the following about this fragment, in the section, *Wisdom is One and Unique*:

> *Zeus is the supreme god. And wisdom is both willing and unwilling to be called the supreme god. It is paradoxical and very difficult for the mind to understand.*
>
> *Buddha says there is no god -- unwilling. Buddha says, "No need to worship me, you find your own light" -- unwilling to declare his wisdom, his consciousness, to be the supreme god. And the next moment he says, "Come and surrender to me" -- the next moment he contradicts himself. Why is it so? -- because a man who has reached, who has arrived, has no ego, so it is difficult for him to claim anything... unwilling. The wisdom is unwilling to declare itself the supreme god, but it is. The ego is not there to claim, but it is so, it is a fact, so it cannot be denied either. So what to do?*
>
> *If a Buddha says, "I am not the supreme god," he is untrue. If he says, "I am the supreme god," it gives a tinge of ego. So what is he supposed to do? Either way there is difficulty. If he says, "I am the god," you may think he is an egoist. If he says, "I am no god at all," it is untrue. So sometimes he says, "Yes, I am"; sometimes he says, "I am not." And you have to find between these two the balance. Somewhere in between he is both. He is not a god because he is no more an ego, there is nobody to claim -- and he is a god precisely because there is no ego, precisely because there is nobody to claim.*

Fragment 33

From Clement, *Stromateis* V, 115, 2.

This fragment can be read with Fragment 49: One man is as ten thousand to me if he be the best.

Fragment 34
From Clement, *Stromateis* V, 115, 3.

Fragment 35
From Clement, *Stromateis,* V, 140, 5.

Fragment 36
From: Clement, *Stromateis,* VI, 17, 1-2.

This fragment hints at the life-sustaining function of the soul, i.e., its life-force, which Heraclitus firmly places as having a part in the cosmos, having birth and death.

Fragment 37
Columella, VIII, 4, 4.

Fragment 38
From Diogenes Laërtius, I, 23.

Fragment 39
From Diogenes Laërtius, I, 88.

Bias of Priene was one of the Seven Sages who lived a generation or two before Heraclitus' time. Bias' most famous sayings was "Most men are bad."

Logos can be understood here as "word" but it can also be translated as "esteem."

This must have included what Bias himself had said, and "he must have succeeded in showing things as they are." (Enrique Hülsz in *Heraclitus on Logos,* Chapter 10 in *Doctrine and Doxography*).

Other famous sayings of Bias are:

Cherish wisdom.

He who cannot bear misfortune is truly misfortunate.

It is a disease of the soul to be enamored of things impossible of attainment.

What is difficult? Nobly to endure a change for the worse.

What is sweet to men? Hope.

Measure life as if you have both a short and long time to live.

Admit the existence of the Gods.

Ascribe your good actions to the Gods.

Studying the fragments of Heraclitus we will see similarities with the maxims of the Seven Sages. Finkelberg points out (page 230) that Heraclitus also approvingly quoted Pittacus, as related to us by Diogenes Laërtius, in i, 76:

> But Heraclitus says that, having had Alcaeus in his power, he [Pittacus] set him free, saying: "Forgiveness is more powerful than vengeance."

Fragment 40

From Diogenes Laërtius, IX, 1.

Fragment 41

Diogenes Laërtius, IX, 1.

Fragment 42

Diogenes Laërtius, IX, 1.

This probably refers to the reciters of the works of Homer and Archilochus and that they should be driven from the stage and flogged!

Fragment 43

From Diogenes Laërtius, IX, 2.

Douse Hubris

Hubris (ὕβριν—the accusative singular form of ὕβρις) in this fragment is often translated as "insolence" or "wanton violence", and understood to relate to some open form of violence, as opposed to an individual act. (See, Marcovich, page 532). This is one of the reasons that this fragment is often seen as having a political side: we should suppress the violence that threatens the community.

About Heraclitus' political views: in *Isonomia and the origins of philosophy*, theorist and philosopher Kōjin Karatani revisits a number of stubborn misconceptions about Greek civilization that have idealized Athens as the center and start of democracy (the Athenocentric understanding that "tribal aristocracies were giving way to democracy" at that time).

Karatani places the origins instead in Ionia and shows that at the time of Heraclitus, Ionian city-states were incorporated and subjugated by the Persians; Ephesus was a city of immigrants that unlike other cities had accepted subjugation by the Persians in order to survive. All this makes a common view of Heraclitus as part of an aristocracy, and a characterization of him as "haughtily denouncing democracy," simply an impossibility. See, Karatani, *Isonomia*, Chapter on Heraclitus, page 80-83.

Turning back to the fragment. Of course, insolence, let alone violence, all starts with us giving permission to our private assumptions and individual arrogance: some judgment or vanity we know better. One of the Delphic maxims was "Do not begin to be insolent"; another "Keep yourself from insolence" (or disrespect or impertinence); and

185

yet another "Despise Insolence." These maxims were well known in Heraclitus' time.

This fragment can be very practical to us as it relates to the greatest maxims of philosophy: "Know Thyself" and "Nothing to Excess."

The temperance we strive for is to live the Stoic ideal of regulating our daily conduct in such a way where we bring our insight in harmony with our actions. Hubris, since the time of the Seven Sages was understood to represent a break with our "νόος" (noos, or nous)—our insight and understanding (and this includes our actions as well).

Solon combined both those great maxims into one single statement when he said:

> *Excess breeds hubris.*

Interestingly, Solon also likened hubris to fire:

> *The beginning, like a fire, arises from little;*
> *Negligible at first,*
> *In the end it is without remedy;*
> *The works of men's arrogance, do not live long.*

Fragment 44

From Diogenes Laërtius, IX, 2.

Fragment 45

From Diogenes Laërtius, IX, 7.

This is the first time in Greek thought where the soul is described as having depth. Heraclitus is not saying that the soul's limits cannot be found at all, but that they cannot be found by "traveling over every way." We are urged to think and seek into a new direction.

Meister Eckhart said:

A vessel that grows as it is filled will never be full. If a bin able to hold a cartload grew while you were dumping your load in it, you could never fill it. The soul is like that: the more it wants the more it is given; the more it receives the more it grows. (Eckhart, from Fragment 1.)

Fragment 46
From Diogenes Laërtius, IX, 7.

Fragment 47
From Diogenes Laërtius, IX, 7.

Fragment 48
From: *Etymologicum Magnum*.

Bios (life) is an old Greek word for bow, so this is a play on written words also.

Fragment 49
Theodorus Prodomus, *Epistulae 1*.

Likely, Heraclitus has in mind the type of person such as Bias, Thales, or Solon. Kahn points out that the number "ten thousand" was frequently used in expressions to indicate "countless" or "innumerable."

Fragment 50
From: Hippolytus, *Refutatio*, IX.9. Hippolytus of Rome was a 3rd Century Christian writer.

The Logos speaks through Heraclitus. It is his and not his at the same time. See also Fragment 114 as this is our task also (We must hold fast to the Logos, in other words to that Divine Presence that communicates to us, and at times through us).

Hülsz writes in *Heraclitus on Logos (Doctrine and Doxography,* Chapter 9, at page 291) that in this fragment:

> *Logos is not reducible to speech, not even to that which is spoken of, but suggests a voice and a continuous presence, perceived but unrecognized by most men.*

Context from Hippolytus:

> *Heraclitus says that all things are one, divided undivided, created uncreated, mortal immortal, reason eternity, father son, God justice. "It is wise for those who hear, not me, but the Universal Reason, to confess that all things are one." And since all do not comprehend this or acknowledge it, he reproves them somewhat as follows: "They do not understand how that which separates unites with itself; it is a harmony of oppositions like that of the bow and of the lyre."* (Fragment 51).

Fragment 51

From: Hippolytus, *Refutatio*, IX, 9, 2.

The bow and the lyre are the instruments of the God Apollo—instruments of life and death. Apollo was the God of the twin processes of healing (including through music, song, the eternal promise of muthos (μυθος, speech-act) in words and in poetry) and of destruction.

Fragment 52

From: Hippolytus, *Refutatio*, IX, 9, 4:

> *That the All is a child and an eternal king of the universe for all eternity he [Heraclitus] says so: 'The life-span is a child at play, playing draughts, the kingship is a child's.'*

Dilcher writes: *The playing child demonstrates the divine ease and facility in doing what is unfeasible to man.* (Page 156).

Finkelberg points out that the game of draughts here was likely a war board-game that had rules, involved calculation and forethought as well as chance but was not a game that only involved pure chance such as the mere throwing of dice. [But "randomness," if it even exists for the Gods, no doubt would be very different from our limited perspective and experience].

Nor should the image of the playing of this cosmic game be seen as an aimless or ruleless children game as often misunderstood in relation to this fragment. Also, note that the creator plays both sides of the game, alone. See, Finkelberg, *Heraclitus and Thales' Conceptual Scheme*, pages 107-109.

Fragment 53
From: Hippolytus, *Refutatio*, IX, 9, 4.

Fragment 54
From: Hippolytus, *Refutatio*, IX, 9, 4.

Fragment 55
From: Hippolytus, *Refutatio*, IX, 9, 5.

Fragment 56
From: Hippolytus, *Refutatio*, IX, 9, 5.

Homer and the Riddle of the Lice

The story of Homer and the riddle of the lice was famous in antiquity. Homer met up with some fisherman, boys in Heraclitus' rendering of the story, who had been fishing, and

Homer asked them what they had done. When they gave the riddle as their answer, Homer, not being able to solve the riddle, was said to have died from grief at that moment.

This fragment has not been given nearly sufficient attention.

None other than Professor G. S. Kirk, who devotes many pages in his paper *The Michigan Alcidamas-Papyrus; Heraclitus Fr. 56d; The Riddle of the Lice* to this fragment and minutely discusses its authenticity, states, after concluding that this is a genuine fragment:

> *And, if the philosophical implications of this story are not at first sight profound, yet it admirably serves Heraclitus' purpose of showing Homer to be a fool.*

This view is unfortunately rather common. Marcovich also writes that the lice-riddle and the boys are introduced only to show that Homer was not a real σοφός (sophos; sage), but not more. (Marcovich, commentary on fragment D56, page 82). Barnes lightly calls this fragment "an old chestnut" and "a little parable" (Barnes, page 58, 76); Sassi also dismisses it as an "apologue minted ad hoc" (Sassi, page 105).

Kahn points out that this is one of the longest complete fragments, and by giving the solution at the outset poses an even deeper riddle why Heraclitus finds this story so significant.

This is in fact a riddle about a riddle, wrapped in a story that is deceptive because its subject matter is so inconspicuous, so easy to brush aside. Or so we could lead ourselves to believe.

First of all, it should be noted that in Heraclitus' fragment there is no mention of Homer's death in relation to this riddle. Likely this aspect of the story is of later date. Neither is there mention of his blindness.

Second, Heraclitus does not have us ponder the lice-riddle itself. He is not putting us in Homer's position of having to figure out what the answer to the boys' riddle was. We already know the answer. The "apparent things," the "obvious," is directly pointed out to us by Heraclitus' rendering of the story: lice is what they caught and left behind; and lice is also what they did not see or catch and so are still carrying with them.

Heraclitus has already moved on and by giving us the answer upfront and eliminating the puzzlement of Homer has us focus on the second riddle: how Homer's inability to realize the answer to the riddle is like our self-deception about apparent, obvious things.

Dilcher writes that all usual beliefs must be reversed:

Men are deceived as they do not realize that their own existence is concerned. They look for something outside, something visible and tangible, and so they do not understand what task is set: not acquiring knowledge, but discovering oneself—which means a process that does not accumulate, but abandons again what it has gained.

(Dilcher, page 26).

See also his *How not to conceive Heraclitean Harmony* (Chapter 9 in *Doctrine and Doxography*, in which he writes (page 274):

The riddle indicates that for Heraclitus it is not any form of introspection that is called for, but rather a different mode of understanding—of oneself as well as of the world one lives in. The boys' action involves not only a reversal of direction by turning to oneself, instead of reaching out into the world.

Here, at this stage of starting to grasp the meaning of this riddle—we have to think differently, look within—it is still tempting to consider our quest for self-knowledge as a search for something valuable we are trying to gain for ourselves, even if this cannot be permanent. To not cling to those fishes that got away, in other words.

Leon Ruiz, for example, writes, building on Dilcher's insight:

> *As we will see, philosophy, for Heraclitus, is a process of grasping truth by insight and then abandoning what was grasped. Knowledge is not, then, a static thing that one keeps with one; it is realization in the moment that one must surrender when the next moment comes.* (Leon Ruiz, page 34).

Dilcher continues:

> *...the crucial point that causes the delusion is that the lice are caught in order to get rid of them. This may appear natural in respect to lice, but it is not natural any more if this action is to serve as the clue for understanding what understanding oneself is about.*

(Dilcher, page 274).

But the act of "catching" something undesirable in order to get rid of it is very much a clue about the discovering or rather the uncovering our self. Self-knowledge *is*, at least in very large part, the result of discarding what it is not ourself, a letting go. We gain by losing.

The picking off of the lice represents the unmasking, the undoing of our false self: that part of us that lives in illusions that we can actually *do* anything at all, such as acquiring self-knowledge and seeing reality as it is, when no such actions are possible for us in our current state. Remember that the fishing boys *thought* they were going to catch some fish, but ended up only seeing and catching *some, but not nearly all*, the lice.

We are constantly self-deluded, especially where it concerns that which is least visible: ourselves. The little destroyers that are on us (in Heraclitus' fragment the word for 'lice' and 'destroy' are from the same root word), and almost a part of us—the lice—can be seen as our many false opinions, our hubris, imaginings, that panoply of judgments, irritations, negativity of all kinds, all gathered over time.

All these are not really ourselves, but it feels close enough that we believe they are. We need to "pick them off" in order to not be completely overwhelmed by them. The sheer number of them makes seeing ourselves, or reality, impossible and does not allow us to walk free. Free from our unquestioned delusions about ourselves: that we are awake instead of asleep and all that flows from that.

With great precision Heraclitus demonstrates the riddle itself—he performs it with this fragment. Yet we cannot accept it. So deep is our oblivion and self-deception.

Self-knowledge is first seeing, then picking off our own lice—one at the time—and it is not a glamorous profession. As mere fisher-boys, we still carry plenty of lice on us, with us wherever we go. We just don't know it yet. We have not seen them yet. And we surely have not caught them yet.

As Dilcher concludes:

Only for those who expect big fish will, whatever they see and take, be and remain a lousy tale. (Dilcher, page 280):

Fragment 57

From: Hippolytus, *Refutatio*, IX, 10, 2.

Fragment 58

From: Hippolytus, *Refutatio* IX, 10, 3

Fragment 59

From: Hippolytus, *Refutatio* IX, 10, 4

The instrument referred to is unclear but according to Professor Kahn seems to have consisted of rollers and spikes or spines perhaps for processing wool and/or can be seen or developed into a machine for torture. Kahn adds:

> At the most allusive but also most meaningful level, this brief text can be understood as a comment on the order of nature and the course of human life. Irrational, cruel, and needlessly destructive as it often appears, this 'twisted' course of events is piloted according to a wise pattern that is — like the course of the elements and the seasonal variations in the sun's path — ultimately to be seen as 'straight' and just. (page 193.)

Fragment 60

From: Hippolytus, *Refutatio* IX, 10, 4.

Kathleen Freeman writes in *The Pre-Socratic Philosophers*, at page 116:

> The Logos is not an arbitrary creator, but a Law, the source of all that is intelligible. It works in the primal fire, and arranges the order of the Upward and Downward Paths, and the 'measure' of their recurrent cycle, for they are 'one and the same' since the process is cyclical and endless.

Fragment 61

From Hippolytus, *Refutatio* IX, 10, 5

Fragments 62

From Hippolytus, *Refutatio* IX, 10, 6.

See Fragment 77.

Fragments 63

From Hippolytus, *Refutatio* IX, 10, 6.

Fragments 64, 65, 66

From Hippolytus, *Refutatio* IX, 10, 7.

Fragment 67

From Hippolytus, *Refutatio* IX, 10, 7.

Osho said about this fragment:

> *Darkness also has beautiful things about it. It is infinite. Light has always a limit; darkness is limitless. And light is, deep down, an excitement, it excites you; darkness is absolutely unexciting. Light is warm, darkness is cool, cool like death, mysterious. Light comes and goes; darkness remains. That's why the Essenes called God the dark, the night, because light comes and goes, darkness remains, darkness is eternal.*
>
> *Light seems to be an episode, it happens. You can arrange for light, but you cannot arrange for darkness; it seems beyond you. You can put on the light, you can put off the light, but you cannot put on the dark and you cannot put off the dark. It seems beyond you -- it is! Light is manageable. If it is dark you can bring light in, but you cannot bring darkness, you cannot manipulate darkness; it is simply beyond control. And you put your light on, but you know that light is momentary. When the fuel is finished the light will go -- but darkness is eternal, it is always there. It exists as if without any cause, uncaused; it was always, it will be always.*
>
> *So the Essenes chose darkness as the symbol of God, but Heraclitus alone chooses both. To choose one extreme is still logical, rational; reason is working. To choose both together is irrational; reason is simply bewildered. God is day and night -- both together, no choice -- winter and summer, war and peace.*
>
> *It will be difficult for people like Tolstoy, Gandhi, Bertrand Russell, if God is war and peace. They think God is peace;*

war is created by men. War is ugly, something the Devil may have invented -- God is peace. Tolstoy cannot agree, a Gandhi cannot agree that God is war also. A Hitler cannot agree that God is peace also; God is war. Nietzsche cannot agree that God is peace also; God is war."

Fragment 67a

From Hisdosus Scholasticus, *De Anima Mundi Platonica*.

Dilcher notes:

> "Now, the soul explicitly emerges as the life-sustaining power in man, together and in one with its faculty of intelligence and purposeful action. Soul is the life of the body in every respect. The web would be nothing without the spider. It needs to be maintained and renewed by its mistress. If deserted, it will rapidly decay. It is useless on its own.
>
> The spider is particularly apt for visualizing the working of the invisible soul. In her web, she possesses as it were, a second body, distinct from herself and yet essentially belonging to her. She thus brings into the open before our eyes an otherwise invisible relation.

See, Dilcher, at p. 82, 83. For an in-depth analysis of its transmission through Cleanthes, see, pp. 181-188.

Fragment 68

From Iamblichus, *De Mysteriis*, I, 11.

Fragment 69

From Iamblichus, *De Mysteriis*, V, 15.

Fragment 70

Iamblichus, *De Anima*, in Stobaeus, II, 1.16

Fragments 71, 72 73, 74
From Marcus Aurelius, IV, 46.

Putting the Crocodile into Torpor

"We should not act and speak like men asleep," Marcus Aurelius writes in his notebook. It is night and he writes by the light of a candle, alone. He finds himself far from home on a strange battleground. His subjects asleep, Marcus keeps watch over his inner self. He reads, reflects, writes. "We should not act and speak like men asleep."

For us now reading his *Meditations* there is no doubt Marcus was able to carry the fruits of his solitary labor into a vastly different world he faced the next day—a world of politics, war, encounters and decisions of all kinds. Philosopher at night, emperor by day—one person and the same person. No one can write what Marcus wrote and not aim to fully live the words.

We measure our inner progress to the degree we can put our understanding into action. This is being and willpower versus mere knowledge. The beginning of self-mastery. Nothing else is of any value. Our being—what we *are* in the circumstances we find ourselves, no matter how mundane or how trying—needs to be infused with the highest understanding from our deepest mediations. Our being then nourishes our understanding and our understanding in turn fuels our being.

Solon of Athens says in one of his poetry fragments:

Take the mid-seat, and be the vessel's guide.

Taking the mid-seat means to occupy the place of the Observer, what the Stoics sometimes call the ruling faculty. Being the captain of one's ship means to exercise whatever control we can muster, steering clear from excesses and dangers from all sides. The dangers are our baser instincts, lower emotions, reactive thinking, runaway imagination. Before we can do anything about it, we need to observe them.

The maxim "Know Thyself" tells us that self-control starts with self-observation, the essential first step for those who love wisdom.

When we begin to observe ourselves we come to the painful realization we are not able to make the changes we so wish to see. We cannot even observe ourselves consistently. Yet, for quite some time we must be content to just observe. We are almost completely helpless in our inability to exert willpower and we must be happy with little and slow progress. We are beginners and if we are honest we must keep that mindset. Solon says: *It is a slow process for all souls to learn and absorb knowledge and wisdom.*

Only constant self-observation can show us where to direct self-discipline—and it can only be done under our own watchful eyes. To be our vessel's guide we need to constantly maintain course between conflicting desires. In practice this often means to choose a middle course, to practice moderation. Nothing to excess.

Aristotle has written at great length in his *Ethics* that virtues can best be seen as a spectrum along which there are excesses or deficiencies on both sides to be avoided. The example of courage — a virtue to be aimed for — has on the one extreme cowardice—a lack of courage—and on the other side an excess of courage leads to recklessness, being a daredevil. Neither extreme is desired, but there is what we know as courage in the middle to aspire to.

We can only maintain course if we are in control. We can only be in control if we observe ourselves and observe ourselves constantly.

How then can we learn to act as captains of our vessel (or stewards) in accordance with our true nature? How do we deal with our lower impulses, prevent arrogance, extremes, excesses? Plotinus, a Neoplatonist, who lived from 204 to 274 CE served as inspiration for a student of mysticism in the following passage, from his so-called *Letter to Flaccus*:

> *The Egyptian priests used to tell us that a single touch with the wing of their holy bird could charm the crocodile into torpor; it is not thus speedily, my dear friend, that the pinions of your soul will have power to still the untamed body. The creature will yield only to watchful, strenuous constancy of habit. Purify your soul from all undue hope and fear about earthly things. Mortify the body, deny self — affections as well as appetites — and the inner eye will begin to exercise its clear and solemn vision.*

The creature, the crocodile, is a very apt description of our lower impulses, our lower self. Like the crocodile, it lives close and low to the ground, oblivious to the beauty and possibilities above. It can never be trusted, and will devour anything that it can without an ounce of remorse or conscience.

The crocodile is that part in us that can never be tamed, petted or made friends with. The best we can achieve will be a state of inaction—a state of hibernation—requiring constant and strenuous watchfulness so it does not continually overpower us. The touch of the holy bird's wing is the charm of the divine wisdom — our insight that we need to put into action—to the test as it were.

Torpor is a state of lethargy or inertness, a state of hibernation for animals such as bears who go into a deep sleep during the winter months. The crocodile is still alive when charmed into its torpor but no longer lethal and in charge. But for the moment only—danger always lurks.

Constant, strenuous watchfulness is required at all times. Pinions are the tips of the feathers of a bird. To mortify means to subdue the body, to restrain our addictions and our unnatural needs and desires by self-denial and discipline.

Fragment 75

From Marcus Aurelius, VI, 42:

> *We all co-work to one end, some knowingly and consciously, others unknowingly, just as Heraclitus, I think, says 'those asleep are workers and co-workers in what comes to pass in the world; different people co-work in different ways.'*

This is a practical Stoic principle. We must be demanding with respect to ourself, yet understanding and forgiving to others. The following words by Heraclitus' contemporary Lao Tsu come to mind here (Tao Te Ching 41):

> *The wise student hears of the Tao and practices it diligently.*
> *The average student hears of the Tao and gives it thought now and again.*
> *The foolish student hears of the Tao and laughs aloud.*
> *If there were no laughter, the Tao would not be what it is.*

Fragment 76

From Plutarch, *De E apud Delphous (The E at Delphi)*, XVIII.

> Context: XVIII. *For we have, really, no part in real being; all mortal nature is in a middle state between becoming and perishing, and presents but an appearance, a faint unstable image, of itself. If you strain the intellect, and wish to grasp this, it is as with water; compress it too much and force it violently into one space as it tries to flow through, and you*

destroy the enveloping substance; even so when the reason tries to follow out too closely the clear truth about each particular thing in a world of phase and change, it is foiled, and rests either on the becoming of that thing or on its perishing; it cannot apprehend anything which abides or really is.

"It is impossible to go into the same river twice," said Heraclitus; no more can you grasp mortal being twice, so as to hold it. So sharp and so swift its change; it scatters and brings together again, nay not again, no nor afterwards; even while it is being formed it fails, it approaches, and it its gone. Hence becoming never ends in being, for the process never leaves off, or is stayed.

From seed it produces, in its constant changes, an embryo, then an infant, then a child; in due order a boy, a young man; then a man, an elderly man, an old man; it undoes the former becomings and the age which has been, to make those which come after. yet we fear (how absurdly!) a single death, we who have died so many deaths, and yet are dying. For it is not only that, as Heraclitus would say, "death of fire is birth of air", and "death of air is birth of water"; the thing is much clearer in our own selves.

The man in his strength is destroyed when the old man comes into being, the young man was destroyed for the man in his strength to be, so the boy for the young man, the babe for the boy. He of yesterday has died unto him of to-day; he of to-day is dying unto him of to-morrow. No one abides, no one is; we that come into being are many, while matter is driven around, and then glides away, about some one appearance and a common mould.

Else how is it, if we remain the same, that the things in which we find pleasure now are different from those of a former time; that we love, hate, admire, and censure different things; that our words are different and our feelings; that our look, our bodily form, our intellect are not the same now as then? If a man does not change, these *various conditions are unnatural; if he does change, he is not the same man. But if he is not the same man, he is not at all; his so-called being is simply change and new birth of man out of man. In our ignorance of what being is, sense falsely tells us that what appears is.*

Plutarch, *De E apud Delphous*, XVIII.

Fragment 77

From Porphyry, *De Antro Nympharum*, 10:

Heraclitus says that for souls it is delight, or death, to become wet and that delight for them is falling into birth; elsewhere he says that we live their death and they live our death. (Fragment 62).

Indulgence, gratifying our desires, is the death of the soul.

Fragment 78, 79

Origen, *Contra Celsum*, VI, 12

Fragment 80

Origen, *Contra Celsum*, VI, 28

Fragment 81

From Philodemus, *Rhetorica*, I.

Fragment 82, 83

Plato, *Hippias Major*, 289.

Fragment 84a and b

From Plotinus, IV, 8, 1.

Fragment 85

From: Plutarch, *Coriolanus*, 22.2.

Solon said: *Excess breeds hubris*

and:

Calm the eager tumult of your hearts. You have forced your way to a surfeit of good things. Confine your swelling thoughts to reasonable bounds.

Fragment 86
From: Plutarch, *Coriolanus*, 38; Clement, *Stromateis*, V 88, 4.

Fragment 87
Plutarch, *De Audiendis Poetis*.

Fragment 88
From Pseudo-Plutarch, *Consolatio ad Apollonium*, 106 D-F.

Fragment 89
From Plutarch, *De Superstitione*, 166C

Fragment 90
From Plutarch, *De E apud Delphous*, 388.

Fragment 91
From Plutarch, *De E apud Delphous*, 392.

> Seneca wrote in *Epistulae Morales ad Lucilium* 58:
>
> *And I, while I say these things are changed, am myself changed. This is what Heraclitus means when he says, into the same river we descend twice and do not descend, for the name of the river remains the same, but the water has flowed on. This in the case of the river is more evident than in case of man, but none the less does the swift course carry us.*

Fragment 92

From Plutarch, *De Pythiae Oraculis*, 397.

Fragment 93

From Plutarch, *De Pythiae Oraculis*, 404.

Fragment 94

From Plutarch, *Moralia, De Exilio,* p. 604:

> Each of the planets, rolling in one sphere, as in an island, preserves its order. "For the sun" says Heraclitus" "will not overstep his bounds, for if he does, the Erinyes, helpers of Justice, will find him out."

Here and in other fragments, e.g., Fragment 100, the Sun is shown to have an intelligence of its own. Here the Sun is exemplified as the Law of Justice, both subject to laws as well as creating laws himself.

Fragment 95

From Plutarch, *Quaestiones Conviviales*, 644F

Fragment 96

The second line is found in Strabo XVI, 26 and Plutarch, *Quaestiones Convivialis* IV, 4, 3.

The Body is the Tomb of the Soul

The first line of this fragment about the body being the tomb of the soul is not part of the DK fragment but is distilled from various fragments that almost certainly refer to Heraclitus through the work of Euripides, Philo, Sextus and Plato. Euripides, Fragment 638:

> *Who knows whether living is really death*
> *And whether death is thought to be living below?*

From Plato's *Gorgias* at 492:

Socrates There is a noble freedom, Callicles, in your way of approaching the argument; for what you say is what the rest of the world think, but do not like to say. And I must beg of you to persevere, that the true rule of human life may become manifest. Tell me then, you say, do you not, that in the rightly-developed man the passions ought not to be controlled, but that we should let them grow to the utmost and somehow or other satisfy them, and that this is virtue?

Callicles Yes; I do.

Socrates Then those who want nothing are not truly said to be happy?

Callicles No indeed, for then stones and dead men would be the happiest of all.

Socrates But surely life according to your view is an awful thing; and indeed I think that Euripides may have been right in saying, *Who knows if life be not death and death life?* and that we are very likely dead; I have heard a philosopher [Heraclitus] say that at this moment we are actually dead, and that the body (soma) is our tomb (sema), and that the part of the soul which is the seat of the desires is liable to be tossed about by words and blown up and down. (Translated by Benjamin Jowett).

From Plato's *Cratylus*, a dialogue between Socrates, Hermogenes and Cratylus:

Hermogenes [...] You know the distinction of soul and body?

Socrates Of course.

Hermogenes Let us endeavour to analyze them like the previous words.

Socrates You want me first of all to examine the natural fitness of the word psyche (soul), and then of the word soma (body)?

Hermogenes Yes.

Socrates If I am to say what occurs to me at the moment, I should imagine that those who first use the name psyche meant to express that the soul when in the body is the source of life, and gives the power of breath and revival (anapsuchon), and when this reviving power fails then the body perishes and dies, and this, if I am not mistaken, they called psyche. But please stay a moment; I fancy that I can discover something which will be more acceptable to the disciples of Euthyphro, for I am afraid that they will scorn this explanation. What do you say to another?

Hermogenes Let me hear.

Socrates What is that which holds and carries and gives life and motion to the entire nature of the body? What else but the soul?

Hermogenes Just that.

Socrates And do you not believe with Anaxagoras, that mind or soul is the ordering and containing principle of all things?

Hermogenes Yes; I do.

Socrates Then you may well call that power phuseche which carries and holds nature (e phusin okei, kai ekei), and this may be refined away into psyche... Certainly; and this derivation is, I think, more scientific than the other.

Socrates It is so; but I cannot help laughing, if I am to suppose that this was the true meaning of the name.

Hermogenes But what shall we say of the next word?

Socrates You mean soma (the body).

Hermogenes Yes.

Socrates That may be variously interpreted; and yet more variously if a little permutation is allowed. For some say that the body is the grave (sema) of the soul which may be thought to be buried in our present life; or again the index of the soul, because the soul gives indications to (semainei) the body; probably the Orphic poets were the inventors of the name, and they were under the impression that the soul is suffering the punishment of sin, and that the body is an enclosure or prison in which the soul is incarcerated, kept safe (soma, sozetai), as the name soma implies, until the penalty is paid; according to this view, not even a letter of the word need be changed. (Translated by Benjamin Jowett).

Fragment 97

From Plutarch, *An Seni Respublica gerenda sit*, 787 C.

Dilcher points out that the choice of the word "recognize" as opposed to "not knowing" shows that the dogs do know the person but erroneously take the person for a stranger (where barking would be helpful) and so indicates a further misbehavior revealing lack of comprehension. (Dilcher, page 24-25).

Fragment 98

From Plutarch, *De Facie in Orbe Lunae*, 943.

Fragment 99

From Plutarch, *Aqua an ignis utilior*, 957.

Fragment 100

From Plutarch, *Quaestiones Platonicae*, 1007.

Fragment 101

From Plutarch, *Adversus Coloten*, 1118C.

Heraclitus seldom uses the word "I" in the fragments. Here is a rare instance. Heraclitus answers the first Delphic command "Know Thyself."

Fragment 101a

From Polybius, XII, 27, 1.

Fragments 102

From: Porphyry, *Quaestiones Homericae*:

> They say that it is unfitting that the sight of wars should please the gods. But it is not so. For noble works delight them, and while wars and battles seem terrible to us, to God they do not seem so. For God in his dispensation of all events, perfects them into a harmony of the whole, just as, indeed, Heraclitus says that to God all things are beautiful and good and right, though men suppose that some are right and others wrong.

Fragments 103

From: Porphyry, *Quaestiones Homericae*.

Fragment 104

From Proclus, *in Alcibiades I*.

See also notes to Fragment 39 where Heraclitus praises Bias of Priene. As noted, the quoted "Most men are bad" is Bias' most famous maxims.

Fragment 105

From Scholia A T, in *Iliad*, XVIII, 25.

Fragment 106
From Plutarch, *Camillus*, 19, 1.

Fragment 107
From Sextus Empiricus, *Adversus Mathematicos*, VII, 126.

The word "barbarous" was used for people who do not spoke the Greek language. The soul cannot make sense out of the impressions taken in via the senses, if it is not schooled in the right language.

Fragment 108
From Stobaeus III, 1, 174.

This fragment seems to belong together with Fragment 41:

Of all whose teachings I have heard, not reaches this:
Recognize how wisdom is different from any other thing.
Because wisdom is the one thing:
To know the will that steers all things through all.

Solon said:

It is most difficult to know the measure of wisdom, which alone holds the end of all things.

Fragment 109 = 95

Fragments 110 through 116
From Stobaeus III, 1, 176-180.

Fragment 112
Knowledge for Heraclitus implies both speech and action.

Fragment 115

The Principle of Transcendence

This fragment (115) is often translated as: "To the soul belongs a logos (sometimes translated as report, principle or ratio), that increases itself." Wheelwright translates this fragment as "Soul has its own principle of growth." We propose that we can perhaps consider the "increasing" aspect — something becoming more than what it already is— not merely as growth but as a transcending of itself. Trancendence is another type of "increase" but of a particular quality, especially where it concerns man's soul.

In life and the world around us we can witness the twin processes of growth and decay at work. Heraclitus refers to them in a number of fragments. But there is another quite different process, that of regeneration, and this process involves a re-creating, a re-engendering, and is what Heraclitus may have had in mind discussing the soul and its potential.

Taken together with Heraclitus statement about the limits of the soul (fragment 45: You will not find out the limits of the soul by going, even if you travel over every way so deep is its logos}, these fragments can easily lead to a reading that what is described as the qualities of the soul describes our soul in its current state as unknowable, and so we have—as we are— infinite possibilities.

The puzzling "increasing itself" aspect in fragment 115 is then perhaps vaguely understood to refer to an almost automatic, limitless expansion of what our souls are made of, i.e., a facile "cosmic interpretation."

Heraclitus is much more definite than that and a key he offers repeatedly is that we should never lose sight of a constant tension or strife, without which nothing comes to pass. We should therefore look for an increasing quality that is not merely happening on its own, but is particular to the *work* of our soul or a cosmos. Thus it must be latent and possible but not automatic and inevitable. Bruno Snell wrote in this regard about this fragment: *"The soul is regarded as a sort of base from which certain developments are possible."* (Snell, *The Discovery of the Mind*, page 19).

If we consider the logos as "sensible reasoning" (see, Dilcher, page 47-49) the increase is then reduced to the process of merely adding to our human intelligence, presumably each time we "think soundly," and make right decisions (all of this, if we could actually do it, already no small feat!).

The "increasing" we are looking for is of our soul, not our functions or faculties such as mere intellectual reasoning. Heraclitus looked within when he went in search of himself (Fragment 101) and there rekindled the Divine Fire of his soul. How are we to understand this?

Man is a cosmos, meaning he has the potential to transcend himself, to recreate, regenerate himself in the image of divinity itself, and so become more than man—a divine being realizing their potential. This self-transcendence is the process which can be seen as the seed that transforms to a plant out of itself. As familiar as this example is to us, it is by no means any less miraculous, just as conception in man. For man transcending himself, to have in effect a second birth, is even much more so.

Going back to our analogy of a seed transforming into a plant, this transcending is not identical to the immediately ensuing process of the plant's (or man's) growth, that process forever and inevitably moving forward to its doom (see Fragment 20) and ultimate decay: the sapling becomes a tree, a baby becomes a child, a child a man, a man an old man, etc. That process of growth is automatic, requires none of the tension and strife Heraclitus makes clear is always and constantly needed, although it is marked by an "increase" in the sense of differentiation and multiplication (of cells, etc.) as well, but for man and his soul the increase that can lead to transformation is of a very different kind, requiring deliberate, sustained watchfulness and pure, directed consciousness.

The possible transformation, or the potential for self-transcendence for our soul, is unlike that of a plant or other organisms. What distinguishes man from other creations is the potential for being aware of himself and of his place in the universe. For all the majestic self-transformations we can observe in nature: the seed turning into a plant; the worm regenerating itself after being cut in half; the butterfly emerging from its cocoon, man has an even more glorious potential—he can transform the seed that is his soul—that spark of stellar essence—to become more than a man: a divine being. It does not and cannot just "happen" but requires the strife, and indeed the war, of raising our attention to pure divine awareness.

This then is the true conception of a new man within us, a re-creation of our self, our soul, in the image of the Divine.

Fragments 116, 117

From Stobaeus III, 5, 6; IV.

Self-recognition is the birthright of all men and our task. This is the earliest reference to the Delphic maxim "Know Thyself."

Fragment 118

From Plutarch, *Romulus* 28.8.4.

Plutarch quotes Pindar: *For the soul alone is from the gods...*

> *...for whence it comes thither it returns, not with the body, but whenever it is most removed and separated from it and becomes completely pure and bare of flesh and holy. For this*

> *is a dry and best soul according to Heraclitus, darting out of the body like lightning out of a cloud.*

> *But a soul which is mingled with the body and is full of the body, like a heavy and misty exhalation, is hard to kindle and carry up.*

Although this fragment is mostly just stated as "a dry soul is wisest and best," according to Finkelberg, the second part ("darting like lightning out of a cloud") is probably also from Heraclitus. (Finkelberg, at page 118).

Fragment 119

Also, Plutarch, *Quaestiones Platonicae* 999 DE.

Heidegger on Heraclitus, Gods and the stove:

> *The saying of Heraclitus (Fragment 119) goes: ethos anthropo daimon. This is usually translated: "A man's character is his daimon." This translation thinks in a modern way, not a Greek one. Ethos means abode, dwelling place. The word names the open region in which the human being dwells. The open region of this abode allows what pertains to the essence of the human being, and what in thus arriving resides in nearness to him, to appear.*

> *The abode of the human being contains and preserves the advent of what belongs to the human being in his essence. According to Heraclitus's phrase this is daimon, the god. The fragment says: The human being dwells, in so far as he is a human being, in the nearness of god.*

Aristotle reports (De partibus animalium, A, 5, 645) this story:

> *Just as what Heraclitus is reported to have said to strangers who wanted to meet him—they were approaching him, but they stopped when they saw that he was warming himself by the fire in the kitchen; but he told them not to hesitate but to enter, saying to them, "For there are gods here too."*

Fragment 120

From Strabo I:

> *And Heraclitus, better and more Homerically, naming in like manner the Bear instead of the northern circle, says, "The limits of the evening and morning are the Bear, and opposite the Bear, the bounds of bright Zeus." For the northern circle is the boundary of rising and setting, not the Bear.*

The Bear designates Ursa Major (Great Bear), as Kahn points out, the general mark for the celestial pole and hence for the North. (Kahn, page 162).

Fragment 121

Strabo XIV, 25; also Diogenes Laërtius, IX, 2.

Fragment 122

Suidas: Heraclitus used the word ἀγχιβασίην—a "coming near to," or "stepping near."

There is no context to help us but perhaps it can be seen as that continual beginning we have to engage in, no matter the weariness (Fragment 84b)—a stepping up to the plate, as it were.

Fragment 123

From Philo, *Quaestiones et Solutiones in Genesim*, IV, 1.

Fragment 124

From: Theophrastus, *Metaphysica* 15.

Fragment 125

From: Theophrastus, *De Vertigne* 9.

This fragment is about a barley drink with wine and cheese in it that would separate if it's not continually stirred. Thus **it stands still by moving**.

Fragment 125a

From Tzetzes, *Commentaries (on Arisotophanes)*.

Fragment 126

From Tzetzes, *Scholia ad Exegesin in Iliadem*, p. 126.

Fragment 129

From Diogenes Laërtius, VIII, 6.

Fragment A5

Simplicius, *In Physicorum*, 23, 38.

Fragment A13

Fragment from Censorinus, *De Die Natali XVIII* (Chapter on The Great Year):

> There is also a year which Aristotle calls Perfect, rather than Great, which is formed by the revolution of the sun, of the moon and of the five planets, when they all come at the same time to the celestial point from which they started together. This year has a great winter called by the Greeks the Inundation and by the Latins The Deluge; it has also a summer which the Greeks call the Conflagration of the world.

> The world is supposed to have been by turns deluged or on fire at each of these epochs. According to the opinion of Aristarchus this year was composed of 2484 solar years; according to Arestes of Dyrrachium, it was 5552 years; according to Heraclitus and Linus it was 10,800; according to Dion it was 10,884; according to Orpheus it was 10,020

years; and according to Cassandrus it was 3,600,000 years. Others have thought it infinite; and that it would never recur.

According to Marcovich, possibly a number that has an origin in Babylonian astronomical measuring, as "[u]sually the figure 10,800 is interpreted as 360 days x 30 years" (which is likely to be one human generation according to Heraclitus), as a 'world-generation' (Marcovich, page 347).

Fragment A15

From Aristotle, *De Anima (On the Soul)*, I, 2, 405

Fragment A19

From Plutarch, *De Defectu Oraculorum*, 415E and Censorinus, *De Die Natali*, 17, 2

Fragment A22

From: Aristotle, *Eudemian Ethics*, VII, 1.

Fragment A23

From Polybius, IV, 40, 2.

Fragment not numbered in DK

From Macrobius, *Somnium Scipiones (Dream of Scipio)*, 14, 19.

Macrobius, a Neoplatonist from the Fifth Century (CE), summarizes the concept of the soul as related by different philosophers:

Plato calls it "that which moves itself"

Xenocrates "the self-moving number"

Aristotle "entelechy," i.e., something carrying its purpose (its goal) within itself

Pythagoras and Philolaus "harmony"

Posidonius "idea"

Asclepiades "concurrent exercitation of the five senses"

Hippocrates "subtle pneuma that is distributed throughout the whole body"

Heraclides Ponticus "light"

Heraclitus "spark of the stellar essence"

Zeno "condensed spirit in the body"

Democritus "spirit between the atoms, so mobile that it penetrates every body"

Critolaus "originating in the quintessence"

Hipparchus "fire"

Anaximenes "air"

Empedocles and Critias "blood"

Parmenides "originating in earth and fire"

Epicurus "a kind of mixture of fire, air, and spirit."

Macrobius notes:

For all these philosophers, the soul is immaterial and immortal.

Ω

Further Reading

Bolded are books that have been most helpful here.

Athanassakis, Apostolos N., *Hesiod: Theogony; Works and Days; Shield*, Baltimore, Maryland: The Johns Hopkins University Press, 1983.

Barnes, Jonathan, *The Presocratic Philosophers*, London, Boston, Melbourne and Henley: Routledge & Kegan Paul, 1982.

Beerden, Kim, *Worlds Full of Signs: Ancient Greek Divination in Context*, Leiden, Boston, Brill 2013.

A few short passages:

Divination was omnipresent in the ancient world: "If the ancient Mediterranean world was full of gods it was full of their messages as well." The mindset of ancient individuals might even be described as a state of "omen-mindedness", as is testified by the amount and nature of the ancient evidence. (page 9).

The occurrence of spontaneous signs was based on an existing reciprocal relationship between the humans and the supernatural. The supernatural was thought to provide a sign voluntarily and because it wanted to. Everyone enjoyed such a reciprocal relationship with the supernatural: this includes women, slaves and children of all ages.

The individual had already established a relationship with the supernatural by giving a gift beforehand, or was going to do so at some point in the future. The preexistence of these relationships means that everyone could receive a spontaneous sign without giving the supernatural a particular gift in exchange for the sign. (page 111– footnotes omitted).

Bowra, C. M., *The Greek Experience*, London: Sphere Books, 1973 (Cardinal Edition).

Bran, Eva, *The Logos of Heraclitus: The First Philosopher of the West on its Most Interesting Term*, Philadelphia, Pennsylvania: Paul Dry Books, 2011.

Burnet, John, *Greek Philosophy (I): Thales to Plato*, London: MacMillan and Co., 1924.

Burnet, *Early Greek Philosophy*, London: Adam & Charles Black, 4th Ed. (1952)

Chitwood, Ava, *Death by Philosophy: The Biographical Tradition in the Life and Death of the Archaic Philosophers Empedocles, Heraclitus, and Democritus*, Ann Harbor, Michigan: The University of Michigan Press, 2004.

Conche, Marcel, *Héraclite: Fragments*, Paris, Presses Universitaires de France, 1986.

Diels, Hermann and Kranz, Walther, *Die Fragmente der Vorsokratiker*, Hildesheim, 1951-2 (6th Edition).

The works of Presocratics are normally referred to by DK numbers. In Diels-Kranz, each author is assigned a number, and within that author's number, entries are divided into three groups labeled alphabetically:

1. *testimonia:* ancient accounts of the authors' life and doctrines.

2. *ipsissima verba* (literally, exact words, sometimes also termed "fragments"): the exact words of the author.

3. *imitations:* works which take the author as a model.

Dilcher, Roman, *Studies in Heraclitus*, Germany, Hildesheim: Georg Olms, 1995.

This book contains many gems of insight, explained with exquisite, rigorous mastery that makes it so worth reading and re-reading. Unfortunately, this book appears hard to find currently, but it is generally available in most University libraries.

—, *How not to conceive Heraclitean Harmony*. **This is Chapter 9 in** *Doctrine and Doxography: Studies on Heraclitus and Pythagoras* **(See below under Sider).**

Dillon, Matthew, *Omens and Oracles: divination in ancient Greece*, New York: Routledge, 2017.

> [Alexander the Great's] *birth was marked by the destruction by fire of Artemis' temple at Ephesus on 21 July 356 BC through the arson of one Herostratos.* (page 205).

> *Divination was not only of importance in military or political crises, but underpinned all decision-making in the Greek world: 'Those who intend to manage households or cities as well,' Socrates considered, 'require divination (mantike) ... What is not clear to mortals they should attempt to learn from the gods by divination, for the gods grant a sign to him whom they view favorably'. Divination therefore lay at the heart of the oikos (household), as well as of the polis (city): the two basic, indispensable institutions of the Greek world.* (page 11).

> *Although Zeus had major prophetic centres, Apollo was the main oracular deity of ancient Greece, and his oracles were found throughout Asia Minor, mainland Greece and on the Aegean island of Delos.* (page 337).

Dodds, E. R., *The Greeks and the Irrational*, **Berkeley: University of California Press, 1951.**

Finkelberg, Aryeh, *Heraclitus and Thales' Conceptual Scheme: A Historical Study*, **Leiden | Boston: Brill, 2017.**

This is an extraordinarily rich work that, like Dilcher's writings, can be revisited over and over and for thoroughness, clarity and depth is unsurpassed. In an Appendix analyzing Marcus Aurelius' quotes of Heraclitus,

Finkelberg dismantles the oft-repeated (and rather glib) assertion that Marcus Aurelius' memory was not very accurate. His fresh perspective on the *Logos* is referenced in the *Note on the Logos* and we are much indebted to his insights.

Flower, Michael Attyah, *The Seer in Ancient Greece,* **Berkeley: University of California Press, 2008.**

A few helpful passages:

> *When the Pythia so wished, she was capable of giving explicit advice in plain language. But when she was dealing with a particularly difficult or delicate problem, she composed verse responses in which were embedded a variety of possible recommendations and a range of possible consequences.*

> *The purpose of such ambiguity, or interpretative polyvalence, was not evasion. For ambiguity is not necessarily evasive. Rather, oracular ambiguity served to define the limits of the problem and the range of possible solutions, and then to refer the problem back to the inquirer. The inquirer, through the act of interpretation, then provided his own answer. But it must be stressed that this answer was not the only possible answer, because many such oracles were open to being interpreted in different ways.* (pages 234-235).

Freeman, Kathleen, *The Pre-Socratic Philosophers: A Companion to Diels, Fragmente der Vorsokratiker,* **Oxford: Alden Press, 1946.**

This companion book, has an overview of all the presocratic philosophers' fragments. It also describes doubtful and deleted fragments. About Heraclitus, Freeman concludes:

> *The influence of Heraclitus on all subsequent philosophy cannot be over-estimated.*

Graham, Daniel W., *The Texts of Early Greek Philosophy: The Complete Fragments and Selected Testimonies of the Major Presocratics*, New York: Cambridge University Press, 2010.

Gregory, Andrew, *The Presocratics and the Supernatural: Magic, Philosophy and Science in Early Greece*, New York: Bloomsbury Publishing, Plc., 2013.

Heidegger, Martin and Fink, Eugen (Transl. Seibert, Charles H.), *Heraclitus Seminar*, Evanston, Illinois: Northwestern University Press, 1970.

Hussey, Edward, *The Presocratics*, London: Duckworth, 1972. This book offers an excellent introduction to the Presocratics.

Jaeger, Werner W., *Paideia: the Ideals of Greek Culture, Vol. I—Book One: Archaic Greece, Book Two: the Mind of Athens; Vol. II—Book Three: In Search of the Divine Centre; Vol. III—Book Four: The Conflict of Cultural Ideas in the Age of Plato* (Translated from the Second German Edition by Highet, Gilbert), Oxford: Basil Blackwell, 1945 (first English edition of Vol. I—1939).

These books offer timeless, deep insight.

Jaeger, Werner W., *The Theology of the Early Greek Philosophers: The Gifford Lectures*, (transl. Edward S. Robinson) Westport, Oxford: University Press, 1960 (first published 1947 at the Clarendon Press, London).

This book is based on a series of lectures on the development of Greek cosmological thought.

> From Chapter I: *The Theology of the Greek Thinkers*:
>
> *Philosophical thought is much more closely and indissolubly bound up with its history than are the special sciences with theirs. One might perhaps say that the relation between modern and ancient philosophy is more comparable to that between the works of the poets of our*

own time and the great classical poems of the past. For here again it is from the immortality of past greatness that the new creation draws its vital breath.

Philosophical assertions about the divine are to be found in pre-Platonic thinkers from the very first.

In later Greek philosophy, which is much more systematically worked out, theology is so clearly distinguished from the other branches of thought that it is easy to give it separate treatment. But in the oldest Greek thought there is no such differentiation....If we really hope to understand the isolated utterances of Anaximander or Heraclitus on God or 'the Divine', we must always take their philosophy as a whole, as an indivisible organism, never considering the theological components apart from the physical or ontological.

From Chapter VII: *Heraclitus*

Let us begin by examining the peculiar stylistic form of the Heraclitean fragments. There is simply nothing with which their style can be compared...Heraclitus is the creator of a new philosophical style tremendously effective in its incisiveness and lapidary power of formulation. It is true that except for the opening passages we possess no extensive portions of his book, but only isolated sentences. Their terse and rounded phrasing, however, makes us suspect that it is not by accident that Heraclitus teachings have come down to us in a surprisingly large number of sentences of this sort. Either his whole book was written in this form, or it must have been particularly rich in such utterances, so that those who made use of it later were tempted to convert his capital into small change.

It is evident, therefore, that his teachings are meant to influence men's practical conduct as well. ... Heraclitus is the first thinker who not only wishes to know the truth but also holds that this knowledge will renew men's lives. In his image of the waker and the sleeper he makes quite plain what he expects his logos to contribute. He has no desire to be another Prometheus, teaching men new and more ingenious methods of reaching their ultimate goals; he hopes rather to make them capable of leading their lives fully awake and aware of the logos according to which all things occur.

Kahn, Charles H., *The Art and Thought of Heraclitus: An Edition of the Fragments with Translation and Commentary*, Cambridge: Cambridge University Press, 1979.

This book is already a classic and no doubt a "must" for everyone who loves to dive deep into each individual fragment. The tremendous amount of research by Professor Kahn offers so many gems. (Note: there is also a Kindle version of this book, which, due to its structure, is in our view rather difficult to use).

An excerpt from *On reading Heraclitus*:

> *It has been noted that every age and philosophical perspective, from Cratylus to the Neoplatonists and the fathers of the Church, projected its own meaning and its own preoccupations onto the text of Heraclitus. ...*

> *By the ambivalent and enigmatic quality of his utterance he lends himself as few authors do to the free play of interpretation. So it has often seemed that the task of modern scholarship was simply to undo the work of history: to strip away the various levels of exegesis and distortion deposited by the centuries, in order to recover the original meaning of the preserved text. ...*

> *[] In principle the effort to recover the authentic Heraclitus, that is, to attain a uniquely correct interpretation, is an enterprise that can never succeed. We are not only confronted with the warning of the onion: if we peel off all the layers of interpretation there may be nothing left, or nothing of any interest. There is the more fundamental problem that we are also historical beings with a certain*

> *perspective, who can only see what is visible from where we happen to be standing.*
>
> *By induction we may be sure that the next generation, even the next perceptive reader of Heraclitus, will be able to see something new and different.* (page 87).

Karatani, Kōjin, *Isonomia and the origins of philosophy*, Durham: Duke University Press, 2017 (English translation of 2012 book).

Kirk, G. S., *The Michigan Alcidamas-Papyrus; Heraclitus Fr. 56D; The Riddle of the Lice*, The Classical Quarterly, 1950, Vol. 44(3-4), pages 149-167.

Kirk, G. S., Raven, J. E., Schofield, M., *The Presocratic Philosophers—A Critical History with a Selection of Texts*, Cambridge: Cambridge University Press, 1983.

Kingsley, Peter, *Ancient Philosophy, Mystery, and Magic: Empedocles and Pythagorean Tradition*, Oxford: Clarendon Press, 1995.

Kingsley, Peter, *Reality*, Inverness, California: Golden Sufi Center 2003.

This is a work of art unlike any other books on this list. It takes us on an inner journey with Parmenides, a contemporary of Heraclitus, and Empdocles. A few short excerpts:

> *It could be said that this process of awakening is profoundly healing. It is. The only trouble with saying this is that we've come to have such a superficial idea of healing. For most of us, healing is what makes us comfortable and eases the pain. It is what softens, protects us. And yet what we want to be healed of is often what will heal us if we can stand the discomfort and the pain.*

We are human beings, endowed with an incredible dignity; but there's nothing more undignified than forgetting our greatness and clutching at straws.

This life of the senses can never fulfill us, even though the whole world will tell us the opposite.

It's quite an achievement. We've actually succeeded in creating the illusion that we're wiser than people used to be. As for those philosopher figures who stand in the distant past at the beginnings of western culture, we've learned to excuse them—to make allowances for the way they failed to draw the conclusions we think they should have drawn. And yet the only allowances we need to make are for ourselves. We're in no position at all to judge those philosophers: they're our judges. When we close the door on them, we're only closing the door on ourselves.

To understand what the goddess is saying you have to keep a firm grip on yourself, not allow your mind to wander. And to learn this can take years.

...

Empedocles knows his way around eternity like a wild cat around its lair. He defines his ground with the clarity of someone whose eyes see straight into another world—and with the faultless consistency that only a true sorcerer has the power to value or understand.

[Empedocles] is not saying he is in exile because he trusted in Strife. He is saying the exact reverse, that he trusts in Strife because he is in exile.

And he is placing his trust in strife, mad Strife, to get him out of this appalling situation he has been thrown into.

Naturally, though, the prospect of him or anyone trusting in something as untrustworthy and utterly dangerous as Strife is horrifying. It runs counter to all our normal expectations. So what he says has, for around the last two thousand years, been changed, completely inverted.

You will note how open he is about the fact that he is trusting in Strife.

But because this is not what we want to hear, we don't hear it. This is not what we are accustomed to because it flies in the face of too much. He gently caresses us with his meaning. And yet his caress is like being touched by a wild animal—something we are not able to tolerate.

Empedocles lays everything out on the table; hides nothing; is totally honest. And no one notices.

...

[Empedocles'] first instruction to Pausanias is not to perceive but to perceive that he is perceiving—to watch the perceptive process itself. In other words he is telling him not just to look or touch or hear but to look and touch while fully conscious of looking and touching, to hear with the awareness that he is hearing.

And anyone who starts to do this seriously will begin to become aware that what passes for ordinary human existence is nothing but a dream.

For Empedocles, exactly as for Parmenides, one of the most extraordinary facts about human existence is that people appear to be such creatures of the senses and yet never use their senses at all. They are just used by them—bashed around by them, buffeted here and there. And the worst aspect of this situation is the way we manage to believe, like blind people so blind they think they are not blind, that we can see the whole.

Leon Ruiz, Nicolas E., *Heraclitus and the Work of Awakening,* **Doctoral Thesis, Stony Brook University, 2007.**

This thesis, available through university online libraries, stands out by considering Heraclitus' Fragments (or Works as they are referenced here) as esoteric works with their primary purpose--as the title of his thesis points to—of awakening us. The author understands that reading Heraclitus demands that we embark on that same journey of awakening—that we must "supply ourselves" in the process.

Building on the insights of Kingsley, Kahn and Dilcher, and going considerably deeper than just about all other modern writers on Heraclitus, this is an excellent and deeply touching work in its own right, very much worth reading and re-reading, and we can only hope that this author one day will offer us more of his insights on Heraclitus.

A few short excerpts:

Everyone who writes about Heraclitus will make at least passing reference to his legendary obscurity. Some will talk about the oracular character of his writing. A few go so far as to say that his thought bears the traces of revelation, his expression, of prophecy. This is as far as it goes.

The problem is that this rather metaphorical way of talking about Heraclitus misses the point entirely. His writing was not just obscure, it was esoteric. Heraclitus did not merely employ an oracular mode of expression: he was an oracle. What he said was a revelation and he was its prophet. Heraclitus was far from the early rationalist or primitive scientist he has been made out to be. He was what we today would call a mystic. (page xi).

Long, A. A., *Hellenistic Philosophy: Stoics, Epicureans, Sceptics,* **London: Gerald Duckworth & Company Limited, 1974.**

The Stoics did not make much use of Heraclitus' notion of unity in opposition, though we find traces of this. But they took from him the concept of a logos which directs all things and which is shared by all men.

Above all, the Stoics systematically developed the linguistic and logical implications of a universe directed by logos. (page 146).

Long, A. A., *Stoic Studies*, Cambridge: Cambridge University Press, 1996.

Of particular interest here is Chapter 2, *Heraclitus and Stoicism*, page 35, et seq., which offers, among other considerations of the influence of Heraclitus on Stoicism, a thoughtful analysis of Cleanthes' understanding of Heraclitus, including through Cleanthes' *Hymn to Zeus*.

Manchester, Peter, *The Syntax of Time: The Phenomenology of Time in Greek Physics and Speculative Logic from Iamblichus to Anaximander*, Leiden, Boston: Brill, 2005.

This book seeks a phenomenological recovery of Greek thought about time. It argues that the feature of motion that the word 'time' designates in Greek differs from what modern scholarship has assumed, that the very phenomenon of time has been misidentified for centuries.

From Chapter 5 *Heraclitus and the Need for Time:*

ἀεί always is precisely the time in whose context both are valid at once. Ever-being, ἀεί ὄν, becomes in later writers the (fictitious) etymological meaning of αἰών, or eternity. But... ἀεί always signifies for those same writers the sensible motion in becoming.

The term harbors in itself, therefore the two-dimensionality we have stressed throughout in this study. In Heraclitus, time is not named but evoked, or more perhaps performed by the ἀεί in this sentence. [fragment 1]. Time is what reaches from eternity into time. Time is arrival into itself as the disclosure space of sensible motion, in the intellectual motion by which it produces itself from eternity.

It is time that we encounter in Heraclitus. Yet in his extant texts we find no direct reference to χρόνος, Instead, where we might look for χρόνος, we find αἰών.

Αἰών is duration, lifetime, eon or epoch; it is clearly time-like, and here sometimes even translated as 'time'. Yet it is the ἀεί ὀν of the Logos in Fragment 1. It is the everlasting Fire (Fr.30), that which never sets (Fr. 16), the hidden harmony which prevails everywhere (Fr. 54), the 'togetherness' (Fr. 103) of the All One (Fr. 50).

Mansfield, Jaap, *Studies in Early Greek Philosophy—a Collection of Papers and One Review.* Leiden, Brill, 2018.

[The purpose of the introductions of Parmenides, Empedocles and Heraclitus] *apparently was not the general public but a small and select group. By expressing themselves in enigmatic fashion these authors produce a deliberate blend of the two main functions of the proem distinguished by later authorities: they announce their theme in such a way as to attract attention and create suspense.* (page 43).

Marcovich, M., ***Heraclitus: Greek Text with a Short Commentary,*** **Second Edition, Vol. 2, Sankt Augustin: Academia-Verlag, 2001 (1967-2000).**

Mason, Andrew J., ***Heraclitus' Usage of ὅστις in Fragments DK B 5 and B 27,*** **Phronimon Vol. 15.2.2014, pages 55-68.**

This article was mentioned in relation to Fragment 27. It demonstrates the great precision and Heraclitean thinking we need to read these fragments and how we can think about them.

McCoy, Joe (ed.), *Early Greek Philosophy: The Presocratics and the Emergence of Reason*, Washington, DC: The Catholic University of America Press, 2013.

Osho, *The Hidden Harmony: Talks on Heraclitus*, talks given from 12/21/1974 to 12/31/1974, English Discourse Series (1978).

From Chapter 1:

Heraclitus is a really rare flowering, one of the most highly penetrating souls, one of those souls who become like Everest, the highest peak of the Himalayas. Try to understand him. It is difficult; that's why he is called Heraclitus the Obscure. He is not obscure. To understand him is difficult; to understand him you will need a different type of being -- that is the problem. So it is easy to categorize him as obscure and then forget him.

The sun is there: you can stand in front of the sun with closed eyes and you can say the sun is dark. And sometimes it also happens that you can stand with open eyes before the sun, but the light is so much that your eyes temporarily go blind. The light is too much to bear, it is unbearable; suddenly, darkness. Eyes are open, the sun is there, but the sun is too much for your eyes so you feel darkness. And that is the case -- Heraclitus is not dark. Either you are blind, or your eyes are closed, or there is also the third possibility: when you look at Heraclitus, he is such a luminous being that your eyes simply lose the capacity to see. He is unbearable, the light is too much for you. You are not accustomed to such light so you will need to make a few arrangements before you can understand Heraclitus. And when he is talking he looks as if he is riddling, he looks as if he is enjoying riddles, because he talks in paradoxes.

Polito, Roberto, *The Sceptical Road: Aenesidemus' Appropriation of Heraclitus*, Leiden, Boston: Brill, 2004.

Robinson, Thomas. M., *Heraclitus: Fragments, a Text and Translations with a Commentary*, Toronto: University of Toronto Press, 1987.

Sassi, Maria Michela, *The Beginnings of Philosophy in Greece*, Princeton: Princeton University Press, 2018.

Schönbeck, G.L.J., *Sunbowl or Symbol: Models for the Interpretation of Heraclitus' Sun Notion*, Amsterdam: Elixir Press, 1998.

Sider, David and Obbink, Dirk, *Doctrine and Doxography: Studies on Heraclitus and Pythagoras*, Berlin/Boston: Hubert & Co. GmbH & Co., 2013.

Snell, Bruno, *The Discovery of the Mind in Greek Philosophy and Literature*, New York: Dover 1982 (reprint 1953).

Stahl, William Harris, *Commentary on the Dream of Scipio by [Ambrosius Aurelius Theodosius] Macrobius; Translated with an Introduction and notes,* New York, Columbia University Press, 1990.

An English translation of Macrobius's Commentary on the Dream of Scipio, a discourse on the nature of the cosmos that influenced classical philosophy into the late Middle Ages. Topics discussed include dream lore, Pythagorean arithmetic, the harmony of the spheres, astronomy, geography, and the immortality of the soul.

Tandy, David and Neal, Walter C., *Hesiod's Works and Days: a Translation and Commentary for the Social Sciences*, Berkeley: University of California Press, 1996.

Toynbee, Arnold J., *Greek Historical Thought: From Homer to the Age of Heraclitus*, New York: Mentor Books, 1952.

West, M. L., *Early Greek Philosophy and the Orient*, Oxford: Clarendon Press, 1971.

Wheelwright, Philip, *Heraclitus*, London: Oxford University Press, 1959.

Dedication

To You, the Reader

You are the Sleeper

Rise up

Awake and Be in this Sleepless Night

And become a Wakeful Watcher

Of Living Men and Corpses.

Ω

Printed in Dunstable, United Kingdom